The Process Therapy Model
The Six Personality Types with Adaptations

Taibi Kahler, Ph.D.

Published by Taibi Kahler Associates, Inc.

Dedicated to my wonderful wife and soul mate, Shirl

Acknowledgements:

Robert S. Wert, whose advice and counsel provided greater understanding, precision and clarity to the work.

Pamela G. Smith, whose careful readings tightened the presentation and guaranteed grammatical accuracy.

Phyllis Baltz, for her coordination of the project.

Ron Nierman, for his proofreading.

This is a handbook on the anatomy of personality that therapists and non-therapists alike will find to be an invaluable aid to effective communication and positive change. Because it is grounded in process, clinicians can use Dr. Kahler's Process Therapy Model in conjunction with the therapeutic or counseling approach they otherwise prefer.

The model provides a means of rapidly and accurately assessing personality structure through language and behavioral cues. Dr. Kahler's six Personality Types and the role that each plays in everyone's personality structure are described in detail. The identification of the unique way that each Type perceives the world, combined with knowledge of the Channel, or style of communication, that each prefers, provides a formula for immediately connecting and establishing rapport.

Dr. Kahler's award-winning discoveries of Drivers and Miniscripts provide a second-by-second means of knowing if a person is "open" to how we are speaking, as well as the level of distress the person is experiencing and how the person is likely to sabotage his or her success.

Dr. Kahler identifies the three sequential degrees of distress behavior that are unique to each Personality Type, when that behavior is likely to indicate a Ware Adaptation, and intervention strategies to address that behavior.

Perhaps the most fascinating aspect of the model is the concept of "Phasing" and the Developmental Stages and related Issues that precipitate it. Phase changes are times in which we experience prolonged, intense distress, work through that distress and emerge with a new motivational outlook. The model describes how each Type experiences a Phase change, identifies how best to resolve the struggle and predicts how our motivations will change afterward.

The Process Therapy Model
The Six Personality Types with Adaptations

Distributed by:

Taibi Kahler Associates, Inc.
kahlercom@aristotle.net
www.taibikahlerassociates.com

Library of Congress Control No. 2008902336

ISBN 0-9816565-0-1

Printed in the United States of America

Price: $24.95

Table of Contents

Foreward vii

Introduction: History of the Process Model (1969 – 2007)

Chapter 1.	Permission	1
Chapter 2.	Drivers	3
Chapter 3.	Implications for Life Positions	5
Chapter 4.	The Miniscript	7
Chapter 5.	New Ego State Terminology Needed	8
Chapter 6.	The Miniscript and the Drama Triangle	10
Chapter 7.	Games	11
Chapter 8.	Dissertation and KTASC Research	13
Chapter 9.	Scripts: Life Reflected in a Sentence Pattern	14
Chapter 10.	On the Lecture Circuit	16
Chapter 11.	Six Personality Types	19
Chapter 12.	The "Aha" – Phases	25
Chapter 13.	"Personality Adaptations	30

Unit One: Personality Structure

Chapter 1.	Nature vs. Nurture	36
Chapter 2.	The Unique Characteristics of the Six Personality Types	39
Chapter 3.	The Assessing Matrix	42

Unit Two: How to Connect With Your Client

Chapter 1.	How the Client Views the World	45
Chapter 2.	Talking the Client's Language	53

Chapter 3.   Personality Parts 62
Chapter 4.   Channels 68
Chapter 5.   Channels and Perceptions 76

Unit Three: Drivers: First Degree Distress

Chapter 1.   "Doc, I Can't Take This Floor
                Anymore" 82
Chapter 2.   The Base Thinker Driver: "I Must Be
                Perfect" 84
Chapter 3.   The Base Believer Driver: "You Must
                Be Perfect" 86
Chapter 4.   The Base Feeler Driver: "I Must
                Please" 89
Chapter 5.   The Base Funster Driver: "I Must Try
                Hard" 92
Chapter 6.   The Base Dreamer Driver: "I Must Be
                Strong" 95
Chapter 7.   The Base Doer Driver: "You Must Be
                Strong" 97
Chapter 8.   Transference or Counter Transference? ... 99
Chapter 9.   Assessing With Drivers 100
Chapter 10. Confronting Drivers 101

Unit Four: Scripts

Chapter 1.   Berne's Scripts 103
Chapter 2.   Drivers and Scripts 104
Chapter 3.   Scripts: Process and Content 106

Unit Five: Phases

Chapter 1.   Base and Phase 108
Chapter 2.   Other Floor Phases 109

Unit Six: Psychological Needs

Chapter 1. Berne's Hungers 111
Chapter 2. Psychological Needs and Phases 113

Unit Seven: The Basement: Second Degree Distress

Chapter 1. Base vs. Phase Driver: The Distress
            Sequence 117
Chapter 2. The Teeter-Totter 118
Chapter 3. Just Three Masks 119
Chapter 4. Failure Mechanisms 122
Chapter 5. Warning Signals 137
Chapter 6. Roles 139
Chapter 7. Myths 139
Chapter 8. Cover-up Feelings 141
Chapter 9. Games 142
Chapter 10. Injunctions 144
Chapter 11. Scripts 147
Chapter 12. Meeting Phase Needs Negatively 150
Chapter 13. Intervening at Second Degree 157

Unit Eight: The Cellar: Third Degree Distress

Chapter 1. Dynamics 159
Chapter 2. Depression 159

Unit Nine: Phase Issues

Chapter 1. The Issue is the Key 161
Chapter 2. When Phase Thinkers Don't Feel Sad 164
Chapter 3. When Phase Feelers Don't Feel Angry 168
Chapter 4. When Phase Believers Don't Feel
            Afraid 171
Chapter 5. When Phase Funsters Don't Feel Sorry 173

Chapter 6.   When Phase Dreamers Don't Feel
           Potent 175
Chapter 7.   When Phase Doers Don't Feel Intimate ..   176
Chapter 8.   Phase Cover-up and Authentic
           Emotions 179

Unit Ten: Treating Scripts

Chapter 1.   Scripts With the Therapist 181
Chapter 2.   Negative Psychological Needs 182
Chapter 3.   Phasing 184
Chapter 4.   Individualized Client Homework 184

Unit Eleven: Phase vs. Base Distress

Chapter 1.   Am I Phasing? 186
Chapter 2.   Has an Old Issue Resurfaced from Base
           or Stage? 187
Chapter 3.   Will I Phase Again? 190

Unit Twelve: Issues in Therapy

Chapter 1.   How Thinkers Defend Against Loss 191
Chapter 2.   How Feelers Defend Against Anger 192
Chapter 3.   How Believers Defend Against Fear 192
Chapter 4.   How Dreamers Defend Against
           Autonomy 192
Chapter 5.   How Funsters Defend Against
           Responsibility 193
Chapter 6.   How Doers Defend Against Bonding 193

Unit Thirteen: Personality Development

Chapter 1.   Developmental Stages and Personality
           Structure 195
Chapter 2.   Why Do People Phase? 197

Chapter 3. Infancy: Dreamers and Doers 198
Chapter 4. Toddlerhood: Believers and Thinkers 203
Chapter 5. Preschool: Funsters and Feelers 209
Chapter 6. Chicken or Egg 215

Unit Fourteen: Selecting the Treatment Model to Match the Client's Base and Phase

Chapter 1. Dr. Aaron Beck: Cognitive Therapy (CT) 216
Chapter 2. Dr. Carl Rogers: Rogerian Therapy (RT) 217
Chapter 3. Dr. Albert Ellis: Rational Emotive Behavior Therapy (REBT) 218
Chapter 4. Dr. Fritz Perls: Gestalt Therapy (GT) 220
Chapter 5. Dr. Ogden Lindsley: Behavior Therapy (BT) 222
Chapter 6. Dr. Martin Groder: Asklepieion Program (AP) 223
Chapter 7. Gloria 226

Unit Fifteen: Using the Process Therapy Model Profile Report

Chapter 1. Therapist's Personality Structure 232
Chapter 2. Process: Base and Phase 233
Chapter 3. Connecting 233
Chapter 4. Psychological Needs 234
Chapter 5. Phase Miniscript 235

Unit Sixteen: Earth Calling....

Chapter 1. Predicting What the Astronauts Do 241

Chapter 2. Psychohistory 243

Unit Seventeen: Personality Types, Miniscripts and
                 Adaptations
Chapter 1. The Use of "Adaptation" 250
Chapter 2. The Process Therapy Model Profile 251
Chapter 3. Is the Client Phasing? 251
Chapter 4. The Miniscript as an "Adaptation" 253

Postscript: Training in PTM and Treating
              Adaptations 259
Appendix A-1: Letter from Ian Stewart and Vann
               Joines 261
Appendix A-2: Letter from Michael Brown 263
Appendix B: Email from Sue Geier 264
Appendix C: Lincoln's Gettysburg Address 265
Appendix D: Validation Studies 266
Appendix E: Study Summaries 277
Appendix F: Intervening at Second Degree 283
Person Index 285

Foreward

The Process Therapy Model (PTM) is a model of personality structure and development that identifies how we view the world and why we do what we do. PTM's basic tenet is that each of us is comprised of six Personality Types, each of which reflects character traits, a perceptual filter of the world, a communication style, psychological needs, and a Distress Sequence with a life failure pattern.

The PTM concept of Phasing explains how we remain the "same" person in many ways throughout life, yet might change our primary desires and motivations, as well as our ways of experiencing and manifesting distress.

Distress sequences are categorized into three degrees and are observable second-by-second by focusing on behavioral cues of words, tones, gestures, posture, and facial expressions. I will refer to these as the "behavioral cues" throughout this book.

The PTM therapist's main goals are: 1) to monitor these cues in order to match the client's strongest perception and most used communication style, interaction by interaction; 2) to know the signs of distress in a client, and know how to invite him out of distress into positive behavior; 3) to give a client an individualized Action Plan of how to get psychological needs met on a daily and weekly basis; 4) to know which therapy discipline will best fit each client because of his personality structure; and 5) to know how to identify and treat the underlying issue behind each of six sets of distressed, "masked" behaviors.

Introduction:
History of the Process Model
(1969-2007)

If you have knowledge of the Process Model or Transactional Analysis, you might find this introduction interesting. If you are not familiar with these models, you might want to start reading at Unit One. Also, please bear in mind that the historical diagrams and information set out in this Introduction reflect the state of knowledge at the time of their original publication. Subsequent research has resulted in changes to this information, some minor and some significant.

Chapter 1. Permission

In 1969 I became interested in Transactional Analysis ("TA") while doing an internship with Dr. Edgar "Pete" Stuntz at the Wabash Valley Mental Hospital, just outside of West Lafayette, Indiana. Pete had been trained in psychiatry, and was intrigued by TA, a new approach that focused on observable behaviors and social interactions.

My undergraduate Bachelor of Arts was in English Literature, and my Master of Science was in Child Development and Family Life, both from Purdue University, where I was working on my Doctorate.

Committing to learn more of this model of therapy, Pete invited Dr. Hedges Capers, Sr. to demonstrate how to do TA in a group setting, called a marathon. Hedges was a friend and confidant to the originator of TA, Dr. Eric Berne.

This marathon was life changing for me.

Hedges came to Wabash Valley Mental Hospital to lead this two-day TA marathon. He ended the weekend with an experiential fantasy exercise. He instructed us, "Let's imagine it's five years from now, and we're having a reunion to share all that we have done and felt these past five years." I approached Hedges and said, "We sure have had a wonderful five years together at your institute in La Jolla. I finished my Ph.D., became an ITAA Clinical Member, and have had a few ideas published." I felt scared and searched his eyes for any sign of rebuff. But instead, with a hand on my shoulder and a genuineness in his voice that I will never forget, Hedges said, "Taibi, my friend, we have helped people and thank you for being with me at the institute. And those TA ideas of yours have touched the lives of thousands." That permission was given to me before I was even a Regular Member, let alone before my first inclination of what a driver would be.

I shall never underestimate the power of permissions. Within five years I had my Ph.D., discovered and developed the miniscript therapy model, published a handful of articles, was Guest Editor of the *Transactional Analysis Journal*, member of the Board of Trustees of and a Provisional Teaching Member in the ITAA, and had been Director of Clinical Training for Hedges at his institute for several years.

Just this summer (2007), at the International Transactional Analysis Association Conference in San Francisco, I was told by another graduate student attendee of that same marathon how profound Hedges' permission had been for him in his life as a famous TA personage – fellow Eric Berne Memorial Scientific Award winner – Dr. Richard Erskine.[1]

Chapter Notes:

[1] Erskine, Richard and Marilyn Zalcman. "The Racket System: a model of racket analysis," *Transactional Analysis Journal*, ("*TA Journal*") Jan. 1979.

Chapter 2. Drivers

My interest in TA grew, both as a function of my own personality structure – naturally favoring a cognitive approach – and of a model that was systematized, logical, and observable.

I have always been fortunate to be a keen observer with a knack for seeing how seemingly disparate phenomena actually connect and combine. One day while observing Pete work with patients in a TA therapy group at the hospital, I saw a pattern. No matter if the patient's behavior warranted a diagnosis of psychosis, neurosis, or personality disorder, or merely "normal" maladapted behavior, just prior to their distressed outbursts there was evidence of very brief, defense–like behaviors.

Dr. Berne had emphasized the value of monitoring five behavior cues – words, tones, gestures, postures, and facial expressions – in determining where a person was shifting energy. His identification of three "parts" of the person, called ego states, allowed a behavioral understanding of "where the person was coming from."

By observing these five cues, one could determine if the person was "in" the Parent, the Adult, or the Child ego state. Furthermore, the Parent part could be divided into a Nurturing Parent or a Critical Parent. The Child could be divided into the Free Child and the Adapted Child.[1]

What I had observed were behaviors that lasted less than a few seconds but that always appeared immediately to precede observable behaviors associated with distress. In other words, just before someone would become verbally attacking from a parent-like position, or become vengefully blaming from a child-like position, or show underdog, victim behavior from a child-like position, there would first be evidence of these brief behaviors.

Theoretically, these could be defense mechanisms. In TA jargon they were considered at the time "counterscript" behaviors defending against "script injunctions."

Agreeing with Bernard Chartres, I have often felt the shoulders of a giant beneath me. Berne had quantified behaviors into the five cues. My task was simple: list these five cues as headings on a chart and posit the "defense-like behaviors," listing each word, tone, gesture, posture, and facial expression example when mutually exclusive.

After several weeks of observing video tapes, I had completed my matrix of five defense-like behaviors, with five sets of mutually exclusive behavioral cues, all of which immediately preceded attacking, vengeful, or victim behaviors. I call them "Drivers," from Freud's drive, or basic instinct, to repetitive behavior. They are Be perfect, Please, Try hard, Be strong, and Hurry up.[2]

It has now been 37 years since I discovered these Drivers, and time and research have validated that they are limited to these five:

4

Original Drivers

Projected (Parent) Drivers	Introjected (Child) Drivers
Be perfect (P): Expect Others to be perfect	Be perfect (C): Be perfect for others
Please me (P): Expect others to please	Please you (C): Please others
Be strong (P): Expect others to be strong	Be strong (C): Be strong for others
Try hard (P): Expect others to try hard	Try hard (C): Try hard for others
Hurry Up (P): Expect others to hurry up	Hurry Up (C): Hurry up for others

Several later chapters will be devoted to recognizing and dealing with the Drivers of each of the six unique personality types with which they are associated – the "Personality Types."

Chapter Notes

[1] Berne, Eric. *Games People Play*, Grove Press, New York, 1964.
[2] Kahler, Taibi with Hedges Capers, "The Miniscript." *TA Journal*, January 1974.

Chapter 3. Implications for Life Positions

Dr. Frank Ernst had taken the basic tenet of TA, "I'm OK–You're OK," and conceptualized it into a matrix that Dr. Stephen Karpman suggested he call the OK Corral.[1]

The OK Corral consisted of four quadrants, each one with an acronymic slogan that represents a person's life position. GOW represents for Get On With for "I'm OK–You're OK"; GRO represents Get Rid Of for "I'm OK–You're not OK"; GAF represents Get Away From for "I'm not OK–You're

OK"; and GNW represents Get No Where for "I'm not OK–You're not OK."

Drivers fit nowhere on this matrix because they represented "OK if...." In other words, Drivers are a new life position.[2] I quickly realized that since Drivers precede "I'm OK–You're not OK" and "I'm not OK–You're OK" behaviors and they are not "I'm OK–You're OK" based, Drivers belong on the Corral between the life positions.

I'm Not OK You're OK	I'm OK if	I'm OK You're OK
I'm Not OK You're OK		**You're OK if** I'm OK You're Not OK

Drivers are either "I'm OK–You're OK if you..." or "I'm OK if I ...–You're OK," do not reflect a "Not OK" position, and therefore have no rackets (negative, cover-up feelings). Drivers are conditional OK'ness.

Furthermore, I maintained that there is only one existential life position: "I'm OK–You're OK" and that the other (now) four are behavioral life positions.

Chapter Notes

[1] Ernst, Frank. "The OK Corral," *TA Journal*, October 1971.

[2] Kahler, Taibi. "Drivers: The Key to the Process of Scripts," *TA Journal,* July 1975.

Chapter 4. The Miniscript

After my empirical classification of Drivers, I soon formulated the miniscript theory, which showed sequences of distress (the "Distress Sequences"), starting with the five Drivers.

I continued the use of TA nomenclature for its classification value. The following diagrams were the first representations of the miniscript:[1]

Miniscript

1. Implications for sequences of negative ego

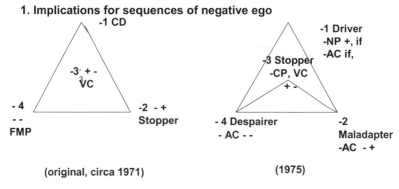

(original, circa 1971)   (1975)

Both diagrams indicate 4 positions, identifiable in sequence by specific ego state terms and behavioral life positions, as observable by the five behavioral cues. First a Driver could be seen, then evidence of a Maladapter ("I'm not OK–You're OK") or the Stopper ("I'm OK–You're not OK"), and then a final possibility of the Despairer ("I'm not OK–You're not OK").

The miniscript was originally conceived to identify only distress patterns and was thought to reflect as many as 60 variations. (PTM has since been validated to show just six such negative miniscript sequences with variations in three different components).

Although colloquially called the miniscript to indicate just negative Distress Sequences, there was also a positive miniscript. My dear friend and mentor, Dr. Capers suggested that in my article I "give people hope" by identifying a positive miniscript. I did so and asked him what terms he would give to the four points. He obliged. The presentation of that positive miniscript, however, proved not to be as valuable in describing personality, as we will see in other chapters. However, it was the beginning of looking at the positives of personality for me.

Chapter Notes

[1] Kahler, Taibi, with Hedges Capers, "The Miniscript," *TA Journal*, January 1974.

Chapter 5. New Ego State Terminology Needed

Continuing my interest in TA, I realized that the discovery of the miniscript had implications for advancing TA in several areas, including diagramming ego states.

Functional analysis was the study of observable ego states by the five behavioral cues. Since I had shown with Drivers and the miniscript that predictable and sequential behaviors occurred, a more precise diagramming of these ego states was needed to explain this functionally.

Since I had postulated that the Drivers could be projected from a Parent ego state ("I'm OK–You're OK if...") or introjected from a Child ego state ("I'm OK if ...–You're

OK"), a more precise diagramming of the parts to these ego states was required. No one had done this as yet.

The Parent had been divided into a Nurturing Parent and a Critical Parent. I further divided it into positive and negative parts for each, giving behavioral cues to match.

As the Adult in functional terms was, by definition, always OK, then there was no purpose in changing it.

The Child was originally diagrammed with a positive part, the Free Child, and an Adapted Child. I divided this Adapted Child into a positive part and a negative part. The negative Adapted part required a further subdividing into four parts: one that showed negative Adapted Child Driver ("I'm OK if ...–You're OK") cues, one that showed negative Adapted Child victim ("I'm not OK–You're OK") cues, one that showed negative Adapted Child despair ("I'm not OK–You're not OK") cues, and one that showed negative Vengeful Child ("I'm OK–You're not OK") cues.[1]

Miniscript

- Implications for sequences of negative ego states: functional analysis.

1st° Driver level (counterscripts)   2nd° Stopper level (script injunctions)

-AC + if
-AC - +
VC
-AC - -

9

Although to the TA purist this was an accurate and valuable insight into the functional diagramming of shifting psychic energy sequences among the ego states, to the casual reader it becomes obvious that there must be a simpler way to diagram this without forcing it into a TA ego states framework. The chapters on the three degrees of distress will show this.

Chapter Notes

[1] Kahler, Taibi. "Structural Analysis," *TA Journal*, July 1975.

Chapter 6. The Miniscript and the Drama Triangle

While writing the miniscript article, I was contacted by one of the most creative individuals I have ever known, Dr. Stephen Karpman. Steve was Editor of the *Transactional Analysis Journal,* and a friend and disciple of Dr. Berne. He had already won one of his two Eric Berne Memorial Scientific Awards[1,2] for the Drama Triangle and offered to help me with editing the article. I felt most honored. He made many valuable suggestions about how the article should be designed. Drama Triangle is a simple, and yet profound, way of determining if/when someone is in a distressed role with another person. Steve identifies three such roles that define the Drama Triangle: Victim, Persecutor, and Rescuer. The "drama" of life when distress is involved can be explained by how we take on these roles with others – by being a Victim and acting helpless, by being a Persecutor and attacking others, or by being a Rescuer and overdoing for others.

As $E=mc^2$ is to Albert Einstein with respect to relativity, so RVP is to Steve Karpman with respect to interactional maladapted behavior.

To Steve's Drama Triangle I corresponded the functional ego states that I had diagrammed, and applied the sequence of the miniscript, to show that interactionally a person would first enter the Drama Triangle in a Rescuer or Victim (of a Rescuer) role, then take on the role of a Persecutor or Victim (of a Persecutor).[3]

Miniscript

Implications for sequences within the Drama Triangle.

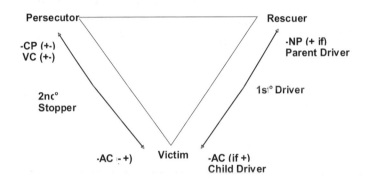

Chapter Notes

[1] Karpman, Stephen. "Fairy Tales and Script Drama Analysis," *Transactional Analysis Bulletin*, April 1968.
[2] Karpman, Stephen. "Options," *TA Journal,* January 1971.
[3] Kahler, Taibi. *Transactional Analysis Revisited,* Human Development Publications, Little Rock, 1978.

Chapter 7. Games

In 1961 Dr. Berne defined games as interactions having an orderly series of transactions, an ulterior aspect, and a payoff.[1] By 1970 he had developed "Formula G," which is $C+G=R{\rightarrow}S{\rightarrow}X{\rightarrow}P$.[2] In the 1974 miniscript article[3] and in depth in my 1978 book, *Transactional Analysis Revisited,*[4] I diagrammed the moves in games using the miniscript, showing that all games start with a Driver at the Con and Gimmick level, and progress to (Second Degree) at the Response, Switch, Crossup, and Payoff, with Payoff possibly lingering as a stamp at Third Degree Distress.

The value of this integration of games into miniscript and now PTM is that clinicians do not need to memorize the dozens and dozens of games to stop the beginning moves in a game.   Instead, the clinician needs only to know how to identify just six Driver behaviors and the appropriate intervention (confrontational) strategies for them.   This will be covered in depth in later chapters.

Miniscript

Implications for Game Analysis: avoid the Driver, stop the game.

Berne's Game formula G:
Con (C) + Gimmick (G) = Response (R) $\rightarrow$ Switch (S) $\rightarrow$ Crossup (X) $\rightarrow$ Payoff (P)
"Why Don't You – Yes But"

(C) Initiator: "I've got a problem, my garage door sticks." [Child Try hard]

(G) Respondent: "Why don't you grease it?" [Parent Try hard]

(R) Initiator: "I would but I have a bad back." [VC]

(G) Respondent: "Why don't you get a carpenter?" [Parent Try Hard]

(R) Initiator: "They charge an arm and a leg." [VC]

(G) and (R) are repeated, until Respondent moves from Driver to
   Stopper, at which time both know a switch (S) has occurred, and
   the Respondent experiences a "moment of confusion", the Crossup (X).

(P) Initiator: ("Ha, ha. You couldn't come up with a solution.") [VC vengefulness]

(P) Respondent: ("That's the last time I give you advice.") [-CP frustration]

Berne, Eric. *Transactional Analysis in Psychotherapy*, Grove Press, New York, 1961.

Chapter Notes

[1] Berne, Eric. *What Do You Say After You Say Hello,* Grove Press, New York, 1972.
[2] Kahler, Taibi, with Hedges Capers, "The Miniscript," *TA   Journal,* January 1974.
[3] Kahler,   Taibi. *Transactional   Analysis   Revisited,*   Humana Development Publications, Little Rock, 1978.

Chapter 8. Dissertation and KTASC Research

In 1972 I received my doctorate from Purdue University. I had created a TA inventory and used it in my research: "Predicting Academic Underachievement in Ninth and Twelfth Grade Males with the Kahler Transactional Analysis Script Checklist" ("1972 Research").[1] Interested in further validating my inventory, I continued to gather data with it. After a sufficiently large enough sample population size, I conducted a factor analysis and asked a statistics professor for his evaluation and interpretation.[2]

I hypothesized that a significant correlation would exist between certain Drivers and ego states, roles, games, and other identifiable distressed behaviors. The results were at first disappointing, in that the strongest correlations were just with Drivers and scripts ("blueprints" of negative life patterns). The statistician, however, pointed out to me that whatever I was researching did have significance. The data naturally fell into six, mutually exclusive clusters at a high enough significance to not be random.

Several years later I realized that these clusters were actually the foundation for PTM to be comprised of six Personality Types.

Chapter Notes

[1] Kahler, Taibi. Dissertation: "Predicting Underachievement in Ninth and Twelfth Grade Males Using the Kahler Transactional Analysis Checklist," Purdue University, 1972.
[2] Kahler, Taibi. "Personality Pattern Inventory Validation Studies," Kahler Communications, Inc., 1982.

Chapter 9.   Scripts: Life Reflected in a Sentence Pattern

In his 1970 book, *Sex in Human Loving*, Dr. Berne identified six scripts or negative "blueprints for life": Never, Always, Until, After, Over and Over, and Open Ended.[1] He offered a thesis and a mythological explanation for each. He did not, however, integrate these scripts with ego states, transactions, roles, distress sequences, games, personality typology or clinical adaptations.

Some of the original TA theorists postulated that the script was a result of script injunctions – negative messages of how to feel or not feel. Yet, no one had researched scripts to find correlations that assist in determining causalities. I had inserted life script items into the 1972 Research study[2] and found stronger correlations between Drivers and scripts than between script injunctions and scripts. This was inconsistent with the postulations of the early script theorists.

Of all his work, I was most fascinated by Berne's explanation and interpretation of the script dynamics of Mrs. Sayers, described in his 1961 book *T.A. in Psychotherapy*.[3] He had analyzed her behavior second-by-second and discovered her whole life script which she had "repeatedly played out over varying lengths of time ranging from a passing moment to several years." How incredible – the "telescoping of a whole script into a few seconds." I felt a personal invitation and challenge from Berne from his words: "After some experience, it is possible to acquire considerable diagnostic acumen in script analysis."

In the summer of 1971, as I attempted to interpret my initial research results, I asked myself a simple question:

"What is it, that is to say that occurs hundreds of times a day, that could reinforce a life script." I smiled, realizing I had "committed" a Be Perfect Driver with the parenthetical, "that is to say that occurs hundreds of times a day." And Eureka! I had the answer!

As we move into Drivers, energy is drained from the Adult, and this affects how we (preconsciously) structure our thoughts, as evidenced by Driver contaminated sentence patterns.

Within hours I hypothesized the sentence patterns of the scripts and verified the significance of the Driver and script combinations in the research data.

I published my findings in articles and books, beginning with the miniscript in 1974.[4] In the 1975 article, "Scripts: Process and Content," I integrated both Drivers and script injunction theories into the development of life scripts, pointing out that Drivers (functional counterscripts) cause the script by altering sentence patterns.[5] These altered sentence patterns reinforce subtly, yet hundreds of times a day, the script theses.

So "counterscript Drivers" cause the formation of the life script. However, script injunctions (at Second Degree Distress) determine how intensely – to what degree of harm – we will play out the script.

In another article in 1975 called "Drivers: The Key to the Process of Scripts," I identified the connections between Drivers, and the resulting sentence patterns and life scripts, which are reflected in the following diagram.[6]

Process Scripts

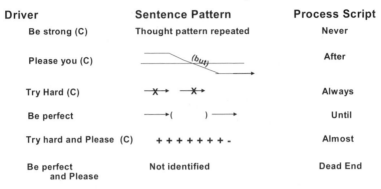

Driver	Sentence Pattern	Process Script
Be strong (C)	Thought pattern repeated	Never
Please you (C)	*(but)*	After
Try Hard (C)	—x→ —x→	Always
Be perfect	——→( ) ——→	Until
Try hard and Please (C)	+ + + + + + -	Almost
Be perfect and Please	Not identified	Dead End

Discovered circa 1971

Current research on these and other scripts is provided and explained in later chapters, including our ability to perform automated identification of each script and personality structure using our online inventory, the Personality Pattern Inventory (the "PPI").

Chapter Notes

[1] Berne, Eric. *Sex in Human Loving*, Simon and Schuster, New York, 1970.
[2] Kahler, Taibi. "Personality Pattern Inventory Validation Studies," Kahler Communications, Inc., 1982.
[3] Berne, Eric. *Transactional Analysis in Psychotherapy,* Grove Press, New York, 1961.
[4] Kahler, Taibi, with Hedges Capers, "The Miniscript," *TA Journal,* January 1974.
[5] Kahler, Taibi. "Scripts: Process and Content," *TA Journal,* July 1975.
[6] Kahler, Taibi. "Drivers: The Key to the Process of Script," *TA Journal,* July 1975.

Chapter 10. On the Lecture Circuit

In the mid-seventies I was lecturing extensively in the US, Mexico, and Europe. More and more I shared with my audiences and colleagues the connections of the drivers, scripts, games, rackets, injunctions, myths, and roles that defined the six clusters of my 1972 Research.[1]

I focused just on these negative behaviors, labeling these six miniscript clusters: Overreactors, Workaholics, Doubters, Manipulators, Disapprovers, and Daydreamers, while adding a seventh (Cyclers) to account for part of the small percentage of the clinical population unaccounted for in my findings.[2]

In 1975, my friend Dr. Paul Ware attended a weeklong seminar in Dulzura, California, along with TA Teaching Member psychiatrist Dr. John O'Hearne, psychiatrists Dr. Stuart Harris and Dr. Ron Boyle from Little Rock, Arkansas, and other TA enthusiasts. Although the focus was on how I was applying the miniscript in treatment, I shared the aforementioned cluster correlations with the participants.

That week changed my life. Stuart and Ron were intrigued with my presentation and asked if I would come to Little Rock one weekend a month for a year to teach them and a group of their clinical colleagues my material. I started my trips to Little Rock in 1976, and by the second visit, I decided to live there.

Yogi Berra said, "If you come to a fork in the road, take it." My "decision" was not based on any logic, which was very unlike me. Rather, I had a strong sense that it was my destiny to move from my condominium overlooking the Pacific in Southern California to Arkansas. And it was. Subsequently, I had two sons, Beau and Jason. I found my life-partner Shirl. I became life-long friends with Ron, Dr. Luther Johnson, and Dr. Robert (Bob) Maris. And in 1984 I met, became friends with, and advisor to Hillary and Bill

Clinton, and I worked with Bill during his governorship, his Presidential campaigns, and his Presidency.

Meanwhile, Paul and I continued our friendship with mutual admiration and respect. He had been trained in medicine and psychiatry by the best and was a gifted therapist.

Paul invited me to conduct a 3-day seminar in Shreveport, Louisiana the following year. Smiling, he told me, "It'll just be for a few of my friends." Hundreds of people attended that 1975 seminar. Paul was very well-known and respected in the South.

Wanting to continue to learn from each other, I returned the following year to observe Paul working with patients in a marathon setting. He was masterful. With each person he would somehow move into their world and know what they needed to experience to grow. What I had been doing by selecting different transactions with different Drivers, he was doing in a different, profound, and effective way.

He saw my wonderment and admiration for his insight and skill and explained what he was doing. "I look for what a patient shows me first, then I decide what to target. A patient is going to show thoughts, feelings, or behaviors in some order."

Seven years later Paul had refined his concept of therapy "doors," and what he called six Adaptations, and wrote an article in the 1983 *Transactional Analysis Journal* entitled Personality Adaptations. This was a milestone contribution to psychotherapy.[3]

Unit 17 describes the work Paul and I are doing now.

Chapter Notes

[1] Kahler, Taibi. "Personality Pattern Inventory Validation Studies," Kahler Communications, Inc., 1982.

[2] Kahler, Taibi. *Process Therapy in Brief,* Human Development Publications, Little Rock, 1978.

[3] Ware, Paul. "Personality Adaptations," *TA Journal,* Jan. 1983.

Chapter 11. Six Personality Types

In 1977 I wrote *Transactional Analysis Revisited* (published in 1978) which showed how I used miniscript patterns in clinical treatment, identifying it as my Process Therapy Model.[1] It was basic TA joined with my discoveries of: the miniscript, Drivers, the Four Myths, sequences of negative ego states, the new behavioral life position of "OK if," the sentence pattern connections of the Drivers causing the scripts, and also my research relating classic TA games, rackets, injunctions, roles, other life positions, and more.

Paul was gracious and in the preface wrote:

Taibi's Process Therapy approach is a powerful way to invite change by focusing on the how of what we are already doing. This concept is useful in all types of psychotherapy, as well as at all levels of communication. The depth and wealth in this book is so great that I have shared only the highlights. I predict that this book will be read again and again, and its kernel, Process Therapy, will become an important contribution to psychology and psychiatry. Taibi is a theorist's theorist.

In that same year, 1977, I wrote a manual (published 1978) called *Process Therapy in Brief*, focusing on these seven miniscript sequences, my "Assessing Matrix," Paul's "thoughts, feelings, and behaviors," and the positive transactions to use in inviting patients out of distress.[2] It was in this manual, that I coined the terms "quadrize," "contactize," and "driverize" in relation to the Assessing Matrix.

The Assessing Matrix

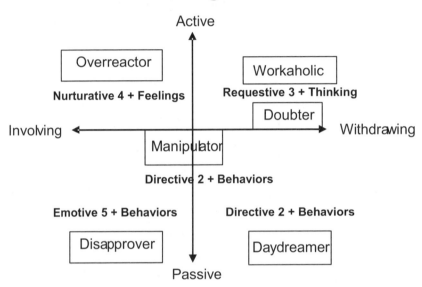

I had created the Assessing Matrix[TM] and placed six of my Personality Types on it, along with how I connected Paul's contact areas to each. In addition, the 1972 Research had confirmed the kind of positive transaction that would be best to use with each type. I called these transactions "Channels" and had names for each. Unit 1, Chapter 8 explains the Assessing Matrix and its use.

Initial Interventions

Adaptation	Channel	Ware's Contact Area
Overreactors	Nurturative 4 (5)	Feelings
Workaholics	Requestive 3 (2)	Thinking
Doubters	Requestive 3	Thinking
Daydreamers	Directive 2	Behaviors
Dissapprovers	Emotive 5 (3)	Behaviors
Manipulator	Directive 2	Behaviors
Cyclers Up	Nurturative 4 (3)	Feelings
Down	Directive 2 (5)	Behaviors

Ware, Paul M.D. Personal communication. ["Personality Adaptations" TAJ 13:1, January 1983]
Kahler,Taibi Ph.D. *Process Therapy in Brief*, Human Development Publications, Little Rock, 1979

The table above included Cyclers, a Personality Type that I no longer referenced thereafter but which is the subject of ongoing research.

Main Life Scripts

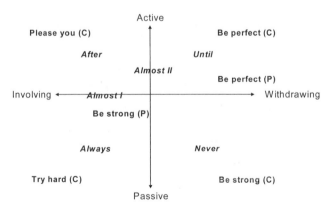

Kahler, Taibi Ph.D. *Process Therapy in Brief*, Human Development Publications, Little Rock, 1979

The foregoing diagram shows where I placed Drivers and main life process scripts (which I refer to in this book as the "Scripts") on the Assessing Matrix.

The following diagrams show how I described each Personality Type in 1977 for its Traits, Drivers, Stoppers, Rackets (cover-up feelings), Games, Scripts, and Dynamics. I also identified the order of Doors for each Type and called these "Levels" of personality. Many of these descriptions were extracted from the 1972 Research data.

My understanding of personality structure was still naïve, in that I was looking at a single type. I had not yet realized that personality structure is comprised of all six Personality Types. But that "aha" was soon in coming.

Active

Overreactors

TRAITS:	Overreactive, dramatic, egocentric, dependent
DRIVERS:	Please you [Try hard, Be strong, Be perfect] *
STOPPERS:	Don't grow up, Don't be important Don't feel what you feel, Don't be straight with your anger, Don't be you
RACKETS:	Sadness, anger, worry, depression, (Gallows)
GAMES:	Stupid, Kick Me, Gee You're Wonderful Professor
SCRIPTS:	After, Almost
DYNAMICS:	Desire: to be nurtured and cared for; set up: Please you invites Rescuer; Payoff: rejection

Brackets indicate any order of secondary Drivers, depending upon presence • of other types.

Involving

Kahler, Taibi Ph.D. *Process Therapy in Brief*, Human Development Publications, Little Rock, 1979

22

Active

Workaholics

TRAITS: Rigid, over conscientious, routine, ritualistic

DRIVERS: Be perfect [Please me, Try hard, Be strong]

STOPPERS: Don't have fun (be a child), Don't feel, Don't enjoy, Don't be close

RACKETS: Anger, triumphant, guilt, righteousness

GAMES: Uproar, Harried, NIGGYSOB, Blemish

DYNAMICS: Desire: wants to be acknowledged and be respected; set up: Persecutor invites Maladaptor or another Persecutor or Blamer; payoff: control or reject and be alone

Withdrawing

Kahler, Taibi Ph.D. *Process Therapy in Brief*, Human Development Publications, Little Rock, 1979

Active

Doubters

TRAITS: Jealous, suspicious, rigid, hypersensitive to negative feedback, controlling

DRIVERS: Be perfect (P), Be strong (C)

Withdrawing

STOPPERS: Don't trust, Don't be close, Don't enjoy, Don't belong

RACKETS: Hurt, fear, anger, rejection, jealousy, depression

GAMES: Corner, Ain't it Awful, Blemish, If it Weren't for You, Uproar

SCRIPTS: Until, Never

DYNAMICS: Desire: wants to enjoy and belong; set up: Persecutor invites Maladaptor and Blamer; payoff: "scaring others" and being left alone

Kahler, Taibi Ph.D. *Process Therapy in Brief*, Human Development Publications, Little Rock, !979

23

Daydreamers

TRAITS: Shy, overly sensitive, introverted, "loner", reclusive, non-competitive

DRIVERS: Be strong (C) [Try hard, Please you]

STOPPERS: Don't make it, Don't be close, Don't feel, Don't grow up, Don't belong, Don't have fun (be a child), {Don't be well or sane}

RACKETS: Unwanted, bored, unloved, hopeless, not worthwhile, depressed, hurt, inadequate

GAMES: Corner, Kick Me, Greenhouse

SCRIPTS: Never, Always

DYNAMICS: Desire: wants to be taken care of; set up: passivity; Be strong, Maladaptor and Despairer invite being left ignored; payoff: scared and left out

Kahler, Taibi Ph.D. *Process Therapy in Brief*, Human Development Publications, Little Rock, 1979

Passive

Involving

Disapprovers

TRAITS: Hostile, stubborn, negative, "frustrating", procrastinator

DRIVERS: Try Hard (C) [Be strong, Be perfect, Please]

STOPPERS: Don't grow up, Don't feel, Don't be close, Don't make it Don't enjoy

RACKETS: Anger, blamefulness, blamelessness, vengeful, vindictive, hurt, jealousy, depression

GAMES: Kick Me, Stupid, Schlemiel, Debtor, Uproar, Yes But, If it Weren't for You, Blemish, Corner

SCRIPTS: Always, Never, Almost I

DYNAMICS: Desire: wants to be nurtured; set up: Try hard invites Be perfect, then moves to Blamer inviting Persecutor: payoff: rejection and righteous indignation

Passive

Kahler, Taibi Ph.D. *Process Therapy in Brief,* Human Development Publications, Little Rock, 1979

24

Manipulators

TRAITS: Low frustration, impulsive, irresponsible, don't learn from mistakes, explosive

Involving   DRIVERS: Be strong [Try Hard, Please you, Be perfect]

STOPPERS: Don't belong, Don't feel grief, anger, fear, Don't trust, Don't be close, Don't make it

RACKETS: Frustration, depression

GAMES: Let's You and Him Fight, Corner, Debtor, Schlimazel, IF it Weren't for You

SCRIPTS: Always, Never, Almost

DYNAMICS: Desire: wants to be loved and be a part; set up: "makes fools of"; payoff: abandonment

Passive

Kahler, Taibi Ph.D. *Process Therapy in Brief*, Human development Publication, Little Rock, 1979

Chapter Notes

[1] Kahler, Taibi. *Transactional Analysis Revisited*, Human Development Publications, Little Rock, 1978.

[2] Kahler, Taibi. *Process Therapy in Brief,* Human Development Publications, Little Rock, 1979.

[3] Kahler, Taibi. *Transactional Analysis Revisited,* Human Development Publications, Little Rock, 1978.

Chapter 12. The "Aha" – Phases

1977 was a year of recognition and discovery. Some very important things happened in my life. First, I received the Eric Berne Memorial Scientific Award for the miniscript and Drivers.[1]

As I was preparing my acceptance speech, I thought of Hedges and his desire that there be emphasis on a positive miniscript. I thought of Paul Ware, who had also focused on the positive behavior of the individual by theorizing sequences of "doors."[2] I also thought of one of my favorite people and idol in TA, fellow EBMSA winner, Dr. John (Jack) Dusay, and his Egogram concept.[3] Although he included negative energy in it, Jack had suggested a positive ordering of ego states. My earlier research had confirmed an order of transactions within an individual, so the pieces began to fit.

I began looking at personality structure as a layering of all six "positive" Personality Types within each individual. I was not just looking at clinical, distressed, or maladaptive behaviors of a single Personality Type, but at all the positive behaviors as well.

I visualized a six-floor house, with a different set of positive personality traits on each floor. I hypothesized what these positive traits would be for each of six Personality Types. I called them Reactors, Workaholics, Persisters, Promoters, Dreamers, and Rebels, as I now wanted more neutral terms, because I was not just focusing on my previous TA clinical miniscript view of them.[4] I began to refer to this visualized structure as the "personality condominium."

The hypothesized traits included: character strengths, positive personality parts and channels of communication, perceptions, environmental preferences, management and interaction styles, habits, facial expressions, home/office preferences, and psychological need motivators.

I was no longer looking at just a single negative pattern of a person clinically, but rather seeing each person as having a personality structure made up of six Personality Types available to him, in some measurable order.

As I contemplated this, I asked myself question after question: Why are people motivated by different psychological needs at different times in their lives? Why doesn't a person's primary Driver ever change even though he might have a different Distress Sequence? Why does a person have a different script at different times in his life? Why do some people demonstrate not just one but two Distress Sequences, depending upon the nature of distress they are under?

As I asked myself these questions, I thought of how many people change throughout their lifetime, as if going through passages – growing from the pain – different in attitude, but same in their basic structure.

I remembered what seemed like different "phases" of my life. As I did, I realized that in each phase I had a different miniscript sequence, as well as different psychological needs, although I was basically the same person.

I had a burst of insight. People start out with the miniscript that matches the first floor of their six-floor condominium. When they don't get the needs of that floor's Personality Type met positively, they show the miniscript of that Type in order to get the same need met negatively.[*]

Research was needed. The timing was perfect. I had been hired by Dr. Terry McGuire, NASA's Lead Psychiatrist for Manned Spaceflight, to work with him in selecting astronauts.

---

[*] Actually this hypothesis was not totally accurate but was fundamentally sound.

I was truly blessed. Terry became a colleague, therapist, confidant, mentor, and a life-long dear friend. I can think of no one I respect more.[*] Terry is the therapist's therapist. He has encyclopedic knowledge of medicine, psychiatry, physiology, and of stress dynamics. In the thirty years we have been friends, I have never seen Terry in the basement of distress with anyone. A most exceptional man.

Hundreds of the best of the best were being interviewed for the astronaut corps, but we needed a more efficient selection process. NASA helped fund a research validation of the Process Communication Model® (PCM) and a "pencil and paper" inventory I developed and was using in our in-person interviews of aspiring astronauts.[5] PCM is a non-clinical communication and management methodology based on my research. This project gave me the opportunity to expand into non-clinical applications, as well as test my hypotheses, and my "pencil and paper" inventory eventually became the PPI.

The research that started in 1979 took several years. By early 1982 the research was completed with remarkable results. Now the 1972 Research made sense. When I went back to it and inserted the new hypothesis, the data became significant at the $>.01$ level.[6] The reason that I did not get the correlational significance in 1972 was that I didn't factor in phasing in life ("Phasing"). For example, only one out of

---

[*] For most admired, I choose my dear friend, Max Cleland, Vietnam veteran, triple amputee, and inspirational hero. With determination of mind and body, heart and soul, he forged his destiny to serve his country again: head of the Veterans Association, Secretary of State of Georgia, and Senator. He is truly "Strong at the Broken Places." Cleland, Max. *Strong at the Broken Places,* Longstreet Press, Marietta 1980. Bless you, bro, and "Hi, ho, Silver. Away."

three people with a Please you driver (basic Reactor Personality Type in PCM, known as Feeler in PTM) will have all of the aforementioned miniscript behaviors because they have not Phased. Two out of three of these Reactors will have Phased, and consequently will have a different Distress Sequence – that of the floor Personality Type of the Phase.

The PPI[7] was validated both for clinical and non-clinical applications. These research findings included confirmation of the six positive Personality Types, each with its own measured amount of energy and order of character strengths, environmental preference, Perception (Berne and Ware's three actually are six), psychological needs, preferred management style, Personality Part, and Channel.

The research also identified the normal management Distress Sequence of the current Phase the individual is in, as well as the "severe" management Distress Sequence of his first floor Base Personality Type. I validated that each Personality Type has a certain psychological need(s), and that when not met positively, the individual will attempt to get the very same need(s) met negatively – with or without awareness. This proved how and why PCM could accurately predict distress behaviors in astronauts and the rest of us. Terry used the Process Model at NASA until his retirement in 1996, in interviewing, selecting, placing, working with, and predicting distress with great accuracy.

Over 700,000 people around the world have been profiled using the PPI, of which over 17,000 have been in a clinical context.

Chapter Notes

[1] Kahler, Taibi, with Hedges Capers, "The Miniscript," *TA Journal*, January 1974.

[2] Ware, Paul. "Personality Adaptation," *TA Journal,* January 1983.
[3] Dusay, John. "Egograms and the 'Constancy Hypothesis,'" *TA Journal,* April 1972.
[4] Kahler, Taibi. *Process Communication Model,* Kahler Communications, Inc., Little Rock, 1982.
[5] *Op. cit.* at 4.
[6] Kahler, Taibi. "Personality Pattern Inventory Validation Studies," Kahler Communications, Inc., 1982.
[7] Kahler, Taibi. "Personality Pattern Inventory," Taibi Kahler Associates, Inc., 1982.

Chapter 13. "Personality Adaptations"

Dr. Paul Ware coined the phrase Personality Adaptations in his 1983 article of the same title.[1] Paul was the first in TA to condense classical diagnostic categories into adaptations, identifying them as: Hysterical, Obsessive-Compulsive, Paranoid, Schizoid, Passive-Aggressive, and Antisocial. Independently, Paul and I wrote of six categories: my frame of reference from miniscript combined with my 1972 Research; his from simplifying classical neuroses, personality disorders, and psychoses nomenclatures into linear adaptations. He included his treatment intervention model of feelings, thoughts, and behaviors for each, but did not identify in his article TA rackets, ego states, games, roles, or any of my terminology of Personality Types, Channels, Script correlations, miniscripts, or the three degrees of distress sequences. He did speculate about Drivers and script injunctions.

Unfortunately, confusion as to the authorship of our independent six typologies arose. Perhaps I contributed to it by lecturing so widely on my Personality Types, including at Joines' Southeast Institute for Group and Family Therapy. However, confusion did arise as was evidenced by an article called, "Using Redecision Therapy with Different Personality Types," by Vann Joines published in the *Transactional Analysis Journal* in 1986.[2] In this article, Vann mistakenly identified "Paul Ware's Personality Adaptations" using my terminology without attribution. For example, "the creative Daydreamer, traditionally called Schizoids...the charming Manipulators, traditionally called Antisocials...the responsible Workaholics, traditionally called Obsessive-Compulsives...the enthusiastic Overreactors, traditionally called Hysterics."

In addition, the article used my nomenclature of Daydreamer, Manipulator, Workaholic, and Overreactor[3] (which would include implications for my research and work in combining miniscripts, rackets, ego states, games, roles, injunctions, scripts, transactions, three degrees of distress) without proper attribution.

Subsequently, in 2002, a book by the title, *Personality Adaptations*, was published, written by Ian Stewart and Joines.[4] There were two significant problems with this referencing. First, the material was outdated by twenty years and did not include my current ideas and research. Second, it does not represent accurately my Process Therapy Model.

I do appreciate the professional response of Stewart and Joines to my calling these errors to their attention, and I wish to thank them publicly for their apologies: for any impression given in the book that they claim originality to my work, including their calling of what they do as their "Process Model," and their acknowledgement that they were referring to my Process Therapy Model. Also, they graciously agreed that any future editions and presentations of the material would contain updated information and credit my work

31

accurately.   See Appendix A-1 for the 2005 letter from Stewart and Joines clarifying these matters.

Paul, and subsequently Stewart and Joines, looked at clients having only three "doors:" behaviors, feelings, and thoughts. PTM research showed that instead there were six mutually exclusive perceptions.   This had significant implications for the treatment plan of what the "target" door would be. Paul now agrees with this conclusion, *i.e.*, each of the six perceptions is associated with one of my Personality Types and this should be considered in "targeting."

PTM also identifies the "Contact door"– we call it the Perception of the Base Personality Type. PTM identifies the "Trap door" as the Perception(s) associated with any of the upper Personality Type floors in the condominium that have a score on the PPI of 20 or less.

Paul had postulated that a person had two dimensions to his personality makeup: a surviving and a performing Adaptation. A person would have a basic survival Adaptation of Schizoid, Antisocial, or Paranoid, because these three were "developed" in the first eighteen months, and they would be observable when the individual had to survive by getting just basic needs met. A person also would have a performing Adaptation of Obsessive-Compulsive, Passive-Aggressive, or Hysterical, because these "developed" between eighteen months and six years, and they would be observable when the individual was performing in response to parental expected behavior and performance.

Although these categories seemed consistent with developmental theory, research does not validate personality structure being constructed in this manner. What I interpret from Paul's insight, however, is the distinction between what

32

PTM describes as Phase (current motivating Personality Type) needs, and Base (foundation, "first floor" Personality Type) needs. A person must get Phase needs met positively in order to function in a healthy way and must depend on getting the Base needs met in order to function.

However, the research has shown that any Personality Type Base can be one of the six Adaptations and any Personality Type can be considered the Phase. With six distinct Personality Types, there are 720 combinations of the basic ordering of a condominium structure. With a Phase possibility on any of the six floors, there are a total of 4,320 possible personality structures, with 36 dual combinations of Base and Phase. Paul now agrees with the PTM presentation.

Still accepting Paul's original developmental surviving and performing postulation, Stewart and Joines, and many other TA theorists, have placed great importance on the influence of the parents regarding script injunctions and Drivers in "forming" the child's personality structure. The implication is that the child survives by "choosing" a Driver to counter the parents' injunctions. However, all the research demonstrates that each Driver is correlated to one and only one Personality Type, irrespective of environmental influences. In other words, every Base Feeler will and does have a Please you Driver, no matter how the parents "script" him with their injunctions. Furthermore, no other Personality Type will have this Driver.

Paul considered the "target" to be the door that indicated what the client needed to strengthen in order to grow. For example, he considered the contact door of the Hysteric to be feelings. He considered the target door to be thoughts. His goal was to help the Hysteric to learn how to think more clearly. He hypothesized that the trap door was behavior.

In PTM, if the client had an Adaptation of Hysteric, then the Personality Type Distress Sequence is that of Feeler. Although it is statistically a good bet that Thoughts are next (about 60% of Feelers have Thinker on the second floor), Believer, Doer, Funster, or Dreamer could be next as well. So taking a one-size fits all approach is not supported. Instead, the clinician should profile the client using the PPI or assess the order of the client's Personality Type floors using PTM techniques.

In PTM, the focus is not on the next floor "door" as the target, but rather the floor in which the client is "stuck." PTM focuses on the floor the Personality Type of which is reflected in distress. The miniscript Distress Sequence of the client will alert the therapist to the issue that needs to be addressed and resolved. Often times this "releases" the person to the next floor through Phasing, providing her with a new motivation in life. As will be discussed in Unit Nine, Chapter Three, the issue for the Hysteric is dealing with anger. If Thinker is the next floor, this will result in the client thinking more clearly, having dealt with the issue of anger. Although most often the next floor, this Thinker floor could have been anywhere in the client's personality structure (condominium).

Paul is currently Chairman of the School of Psychiatry at Louisiana State University Health Services Center. Moreover, in 2007, Paul was honored with a Teacher of the Year Award from the American Psychiatric Association for his outstanding teaching skills and programs for medical students.

Paul and I are currently undertaking a research project of profiling patients with the PPI (which in this context has an output called the Process Therapy Model Profile, or "PTMP"), assessing them by his Adaptations and correlating the results with classical diagnostic categories of the DSM-IV. Then we intend to combine efforts to train professionals in using our approaches in doing psychotherapy and counseling. A therapist can use the PTMP, and learn PTM processing, and then with Paul, or his trained colleagues, learn how to conduct client interviews for classical diagnosis, and how to treat each Adaptation.

Chapter Notes

[1] Ware, Paul. "Personality Adaptations," *TA Journal*, Jan. 1983.

[2] Joines, Vann. "Using Redicision Therapy with Different Personality Types," *TA Journal,* 1986.

[3] Kahler, Taibi. *Process Therapy in Brief,* Human Development Publications, Little Rock, 1979.

[4] Joines, Vann and Ian Stewart, *Personality Adaptations,* Lifespace Publishing, Nottingham, England, 2002.

Unit One
Personality Structure

Individuals are comprised of six Personality Types, called Thinker, Believer, Feeler, Doer, Funster, and Dreamer. My original 1978 names for these PTM types were, respectively: Workaholic, Doubter, Overreactor, Manipulator, Disapprover, and Daydreamer. In the non-clinical Process Communication Model,® the names are, respectively: Workaholic, Persister, Reactor, Promoter, Rebel, and Dreamer.

Chapter 1. Nature vs. Nurture

For years there has been controversy as to how much influence nature has on our personality (what we were born with) and how much influence nurturing has on our personality (what we experience in our environment).

PTM research has shown that there are six distinct personality types (the "Personality Types" or the "Types") and that each individual has characteristics of all six Types.[1] We either are born with one of the six Types as strongest or it becomes strongest very early in life. Test-retest studies indicate that this foundational or "base" Type (the "Base") is almost certain to remain the same throughout a person's entire life.[2]

Research also has shown that the other five Types are found in each person in a distinct order, following the Base. Observations of more than 20,000 children by trained PTM professional Parent Educators in Brevard Community College

Day Care Centers from 1978 to 1996 showed that the order of the other five Personality Types is set by about age seven.[*]

Personality structure can be thought of as a six-floor condominium and I use the terms "structure" and "condominium" interchangeably throughout this work. "Nature" likely is responsible for the first, Base floor, while the order of floors two through six is determined by the environment interacting with natural "temperaments." These "nurture" factors include such variables as: mother and father's personality condominium, developmental stage experiences, presence of other significant individuals, death, divorce, siblings, and injuries and other traumas.

Therefore each person will have a specific ordering of his personality condominium, the uniqueness of which will be 1 in 720 combinations.[†]

The Personality Pattern Inventory (the "PPI") provides this order and the relative amount of energy available on each Personality Type floor.[‡] Energy scores of 40 or more indicate that the person is able to experience and demonstrate the positive characteristics associated with that Personality Type.

---

[*] *See* Appendix B for an email from Dr. Susan Geier, retired head of the department.

[†] *See* Appendix D: Test-retest reliability research suggests that the order of the condominium seldom if ever changes and that any change to a new motivational or "Phase" floor is predictable. *See* Stansbury, Pat. "Report of adherence to theory discovered when the Personality Pattern Inventory was administered twice," Baton Rouge, 1990.

[‡] *See* Chapter 12 of the Introduction for information on the development of the PPI.

By definition all behavior within the condominium is healthy and "OK." No one type is better or worse, or more or less intelligent.[*]

Accessing each floor and the associated positive behaviors of that Personality Type can be accomplished quickly, as long as the individual is "in a good place." This depends upon how well the person's psychological needs are being met.[†]

Personality Condominium

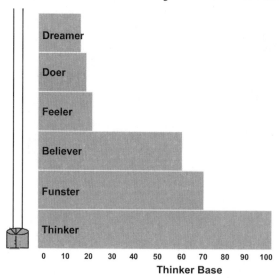

Thinker Base

This personality condominium indicates that the person has a Thinker Base and is relatively open to successive floors

---

[*] It is my belief that further research on these Personality Types and intelligence will enhance our appreciation of natural giftedness and how we define "intelligence."

[†] These are the needs of the person's "Phase" Personality Type. Several chapters of this book are devoted to explaining Phase and the associated motivational psychological needs.

of Funster and Believer. The Dreamer floor is least often visited. Note that there is an "elevator" in the condominium. We use this elevator when we access the floors of our condominium other than the Base.

Each of the Personality Types has associated with it a unique set of characteristics, including a Perception (or way of viewing the world), character strengths, facial features (resulting mostly from repetitive use of expressions) and traits.

Chapter Notes

[1] Kahler, Taibi. Personality Pattern Inventory Validation Studies," Kahler Communications, Inc., 1982.
[2] Stansbury, Pat. "Report of adherence to theory discovered when the Personality Pattern Inventory was administered twice," Baton Rouge, 1990.

Chapter 2. The Unique Characteristics of the Six Personality Types

The following summarizes the unique characteristics of the six Personality Types.[1]

Thinker:

In North America, 25% of the general population are Base Thinkers – 75% men, 25% women.[*] Each of us has a Thinker floor, with an amount of energy available to experience and demonstrate the following:

---

[*] These percentages and those stated for the other Personality Types are approximate and are based on analysis of the almost 400,000 North American PPI results available.

Perception: Thoughts. Identifies and categorizes people and things.

Character strengths: Logical, responsible, and organized.

Facial features: Horizontal lines on forehead.

Traits: Ability to think logically; takes in facts and ideas and synthesizes them.

Believer:

In North America, 10% of the general population are Base Believers – 75% men, 25% women. Each of us has a Believer floor, with an amount of energy available to experience and demonstrate the following:

Perception: Opinions. Judges first by evaluating people and things.

Character strengths: Dedicated, observant, and conscientious.

Facial features: Vertical line(s) between eyes.

Traits: Ability to express opinions, beliefs, judgments.

Feeler:

In North America, 30% of the general population are Base Feelers – 25% men, 75% women. Each of us has a Feeler floor, with an amount of energy available to experience and demonstrate the following:

Perception: Emotions. Takes in people and things by feeling about them.

Character strengths: Compassionate, sensitive, and warm.

Facial features: Half moon lines over eyes.

Traits: Ability to nurture and give to others. Good at creating harmony.

Doer:

In North America, 5% of the general population are Base Doers – 60% men, 40% women. Each of us has a Doer floor, with an amount of energy available to experience and demonstrate the following:

Perception: Actions. Experiences the world by doing.

Character strengths: Charming, adaptable, and persuasive.

Facial features: In Caucasians, ruddy, outdoor complexion.

Traits: Ability to be firm and direct.

Funster:

In North America, 20% of the general population are Base Funsters – 40% men, 60% women. Each of us has a Funster floor, with an amount of energy available to experience and demonstrate the following:

Perception: Reactions. Reacts to people and things with likes and dislikes.

Character strengths: Spontaneous, creative, playful.

Facial features: Smile lines around eyes and mouth.

Traits: Ability to be humorous, play, and enjoy the present.

Dreamer:

In North America, 10% of the general population are Base Dreamers – 40% men, 60% women. Each of us has a Dreamer floor, with an amount of energy available to experience and demonstrate the following:

Perception: Inactions. Motivated into action by people and things.

Character strengths: Reflective, imaginative, calm.

Facial features: Smooth face. Few lines, even with age.

Traits: Ability to see the big picture. Works well with things and directions.

Chapter Notes

[1.] Kahler, Taibi. Process Communication Model, Kahler Communications, Inc., Little Rock, 1982.

Chapter 3. The Assessing Matrix.

The Assessing Matrix is a valuable diagram in visualizing personality dynamics.[1]

The Assessing Matrix

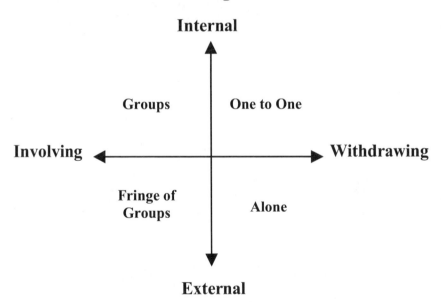

The vertical line is the axis of goal involvement. The horizontal is the axis of people involvement. Internal refers to the amount of investment a person has in setting a goal, or a task, and being self-motivated to its completion. Involving refers to the desire to be in a group or with group effort. A person who prefers to be with two or more people fits to the left of the vertical axis, while a person who prefers to be with one other person or to be alone fits to the right.

A person who fits into the upper left quadrant (internal-involving), upon arrival at a party, is enthusiastic, moves toward people, and enjoys being in groups. In a work setting, this person prefers to work with groups and enjoys projects that are shared with others and that provide involvement and harmony.

At the same party, the person who fits into the upper right quadrant (internal-withdrawing) talks of intellectual matters, but often prefers a contemplative drink solo on the patio, or peruses the host's library. At the office, this person works well alone or with one other person, usually being achievement oriented.

The occupier of the bottom right hand quadrant (external-withdrawing) arrives quietly at the party, avoids people and engages in unnoticed introspection. On the job, this worker is the loner who prefers being given an assignment and left alone to do the work.

The person who fits into the bottom left quadrant (external-involving), likes to party and to be with people, but may need a lot of attention. On the job, this person enjoys being in several groups (teams), but may work best when offered a creative challenge.

When we correlate the Personality Types to the interaction preferences on the Assessing Matrix, we see that the Feeler prefers groups and is people oriented. The Thinker and Believer prefer tasks and are internally motivated. The Dreamer prefers solitude and is externally motivated. Both the Funster and Doer "play it by ear" to see what the environment provides.[2]

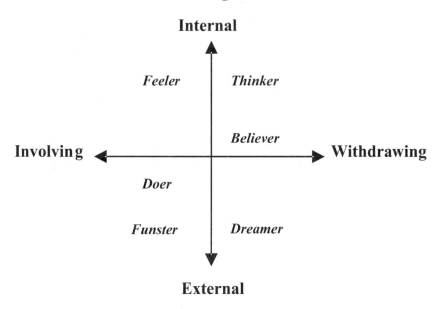

The Assessing Matrix

Internal

Feeler   *Thinker*

Believer

Involving ← → **Withdrawing**

Doer

Funster   *Dreamer*

External

Chapter Notes

[1] Kahler, Taibi. *Process Therapy in Brief,* Human Development Publications, Little Rock, 1979.
[2] *Ibid.*

Unit Two
How to Connect with Your Client

There are two important process elements to consider when connecting with your client: Perceptions and Channels. A Perception is a filter by which we view and interpret the world. A Channel is a positive interaction with an offer and an acceptance.

Chapter 1. How the Client Views the World

Dr. Eric Berne defined ego states as "coherent systems of thought and feeling manifested by corresponding patterns of behavior."[1] Dr. Paul Ware further conceptualized thoughts, feelings, and behaviors as being sequential.[2] He showed the clinical value in determining this order in a patient, matching the strongest of these three in order to make initial contact with the patient (the Open Door), then focusing on the probable growth potential area (the Target Door), and avoiding the last area (the Trap Door).

Paul spoke of these doors of "feelings, thoughts, and behaviors" and identified them as "areas in which each client invests energy." He did not identify them as perceptions, ego states, or transactions. In my 1979 – 1982 research,[3] I found significant correlations between each of the six Personality Types and what I called "Perceptions." The following diagram compares Paul's original model of looking at feelings, thinking, and behavior, and my research findings of Perceptions.

Ware Model		**Kahler Research Findings**
Doors		Perceptions
Feelings	——▶	Emotions
Thoughts	——▶ ——▶	Thoughts Opinions
Behaviors	——▶ ——▶ ——▶	Reactions (likes/dislikes) Inactions (reflections) Actions

In other words, everyone views the world around them in at least six different ways – through their Perceptions of Thoughts, Emotions, Opinions, Inactions (reflections), Actions or Reactions (likes and dislikes).

Not only are these the filters by which we experience the world, these Perceptions become the way we contact others and prefer that they contact us. Each of us has a primary Perception or preference as to *how* we say the content of *what* we are saying. This primary Perception is that of our Base, or first floor, Personality Type.

Thinkers. Those whose primary Perception is Thoughts value facts. The way they view the world is by identifying and categorizing people and things. They prize data and information. Logic is their currency.[*4]

Believers. Those whose primary Perception is Opinions value trust. The way they view the world is by evaluating

---

* "Currency" refers to that which the person uses to get through life.

people and situations through a belief system. They prize loyalty and commitment. Values is their currency.[5]

Feelers. Those whose primary Perception is Emotions value relationships. The way they view the world is by feeling about people and situations. They prize family and friendship. Compassion is their currency.[6]

Dreamers. Those whose primary Perception is Inactions value direction. The way they view the world is by reflecting about what is happening. They prize privacy and their own space. Imagination is their currency.[7]

Funsters. Those whose primary Perception is Reactions value fun. The way they view the world is by reacting to people and situations with likes and dislikes. They prize spontaneity and creativity. Humor is their currency.[8]

Doers. Those whose primary Perception is Actions value initiative. The way they view the world is by experiencing situations and making things happen. They prize adaptability and self-sufficiency. Charm is their currency.[9]

The diagram below illustrates the Personality structure of a Thinker Base client. It also shows how much relative amount of Perception energy he has in each floor.[*]

We can interpret this condominium by looking at the Perceptual language spoken by each floor Personality Type. Since the client's Base Personality Type is a Thinker, we need to move to our Thinker floor and make contact through

---

[*] The PTMP will produce this graph automatically. A PTM trained therapist also can confirm this empirically by shifting into the six perceptions conversationally.

47

Thoughts – focusing our process on facts, data, information, logic, and thinking.

Personality Condominium

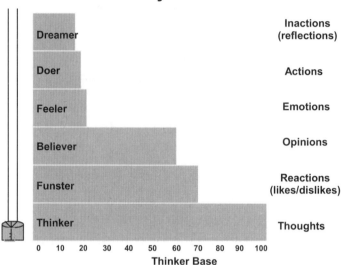

Dreamer		Inactions (reflections)
Doer		Actions
Feeler		Emotions
Believer		Opinions
Funster		Reactions (likes/dislikes)
Thinker		Thoughts

0 10 20 30 40 50 60 70 80 90 100

Thinker Base

This client also has scores above 40 in Reactions (likes/dislikes) and Opinions, indicating that these Perceptions are relatively open. In other words, no matter what the content of discussion is, the client will communicate and "hear" the content using Thoughts, Reactions (likes/dislikes) or even Opinions, with Thoughts the preferred "language."

The Inactions score of less than 20 predicts that the client will not be able to sustain a process of being required to reflect or be introspective.

Every time the therapist or client says something, one of these six Perceptions is utilized. And in order to understand what is being said (the content), we must first understand the language (Perception). Therefore, the therapist must know what language (Perception) the client prefers and the therapist must speak it.

The following will give the reader a beginning template for determining how to classify words into each of six Perceptual languages.[11]

Thinker: Thoughts (logic)

"I think..." "What options..." "Does that mean..."
"Who..." "What..." "When..." "Where..." "...facts"
"...information" "data" "time frames"

Believer: Opinions (values)

"In my opinion..." "We should..." "I believe..."
"...respect" "...values" "...admiration" "...commitment"
"...dedication" "...trust"

Feeler: Emotions (compassion)

"I feel..." "I'm comfortable with..." "I care..." "...happy"
"...sad" "I love..." "...close"

Dreamer: Inactions (reflections)

"Need time to reflect..." "Wait for more direction..."
"Hold back..." "Easy pace..." "Own space..." "Don't
want to rock the boat..."

Funster: Reactions (likes and dislikes)

"Wow..." "I like..." "I don't like [hate]..." "don't want..."
"[fun, slang phrases]"

Doer: Actions (charm)

"Bottom line..." "...best shot" "...make it happen" "Go for it..." "Enough talk..."

Most of us naturally listen to, and favor the content of, what is being said. We filter this content through our favorite Perception, and interpret reality as we "see/hear" it. And from this we draw many conclusions. For example:

The Thinker, filtering with Thoughts: "The secret to success and prosperity is to work hard, think clearly, be logical and structure your time."

The Believer, filtering with Opinions: "The secret to success and prosperity is to be conscientious, follow the rules, and conform to the right standards."

The Feeler, filtering with Emotions: "The secret to success and prosperity is to be giving, loving, considerate of other people's feelings, and be unconditionally accepting."

The Dreamer, filtering with Inactions (reflections): "The secret to success and prosperity is to be reflective and not get overly excited. It is important to get some alone time every day to reflect and be introspective."

The Funster, filtering with Reactions (likes/dislikes): "The secret to success and prosperity is to be yourself, do your own thing, have fun, and be creative."

The Doer, filtering with Actions: "The secret to success and prosperity is to do exciting things, be charming and persuasive, and look out for number one."

The Perception of the person is reflected through his language, but permeates every "how" that he experiences the world. If I say to you, "the Grand Canyon," and you have been there, you know all the implications of the words Grand Canyon. With each Perception, multiply life experiences by the largest number you can, and you approach the different, singular Perceptual ways a person can be convinced of the way the world is.

The magic of speaking Perceptual language is placing oneself into a same world experience, so listening to the language is crucial.

Tuning into the process means listening for *how* someone says *what* he is saying – what Perceptual language the person is speaking.

Practice tuning into a person's process by listening closely to the words (Perceptual language) spoken. Don't be concerned if, at first, you cannot monitor second-by-second because the person will continue to use his favorite Personality Type Base Perceptual language again and again.

The following references from popular culture and history will help you familiarize the Perceptual language for each Base type.[*]

Base	**Perception**	**Character/Person**
Thinker	Thoughts	Descartes
		Joe Friday (Dragnet)
		Spock (Star Trek)
		Data (Star Trek)
		Monica (Friends)

---

[*] Where actors are named, it is the character to whom we are referring, not the actor.

51

Believer	Opinions	Archie Bunker
		Martin Luther King
		Superman
		Lt. Dan (Forrest Gump)
		Colonel Nathan R. Jessup (A
		Few Good Men)
		Sunday Morning Preachers
Feeler	Emotions	Dr. McCoy (Star Trek)
		Rachel (Friends)
		Hoss Cartwright (Bonanza)
		Mr. Rogers
Funster	Reactions	Thomas Edison
	(likes/dislikes)	James Dean
		Lucy Ricardo (I Love Lucy)
		Hawkeye Pierce (M.A.S.H.)
		Robin Williams in: Mrs.
		Doubtfire, Good Morning
		Vietnam, Dead Poet's Society,
		Aladdin.
		Tom Cruise in A Few Good Men
		Calvin (Calvin & Hobbes)
Dreamer	Inactions	Albert Einstein
	(reflections)	Forrest Gump
		Radar O'Reily (M.A.S.H.)
		Charlie Brown
Doer	Actions	James Bond
		Captain Jack Sparrow
		Ferris Bueller
		Richard Gere in An Officer and a
		Gentleman
		Leonardo DiCaprio in Catch Me
		if You Can
		Steve Martin in My Blue Heaven
		and Leap of Faith

Chapter Notes

[1] Berne, Eric. *Games People Play,* Grove Press, New York, 1964.
[2] Ware, Paul. "Personality Adaptations," *TA Journal,* Jan. 1983.
[3] Kahler, Taibi. "Personality Pattern Inventory Validation Studies," Kahler Communications, Inc., 1982.
[4] Kahler, Taibi. *Process Communication Model,* Kahler Communication, Inc., Little Rock, 1982.
[5] *Ibid.*
[6] *Ibid.*
[7] *Ibid.*
[8] *Ibid.*
[9] *Ibid.*
[10] Kahler, Taibi. *Personality Pattern Inventory,* Taibi Kahler Associates, Inc., Little Rock, 1982.
[11] *Op. cit.* at 4.

Chapter 2. Talking the Client's Language

Each of us has a favorite Perception. It is the Perception associated with the Personality Type at the Base of our personality condominium. We are either born with it or develop it very early in life. This Perception acts like a filter, and we advertise it by the words we choose, like "I think" or "I feel." Each time we say something we will be reflecting our Perceptual interpretation of others around us and the world.

To connect with another person, speak his or her Perceptual language. Why? Because process precedes content. First I need to speak a foreign language in order for the non-English speaking person to understand what I am saying in content.

Empirical research has shown that if we do not connect in Perception with another person, distress often results.

The following diagrams show a Feeler wife and a Thinker husband. The wife could have been a Thinker (one in four are female), and the husband could have been a Feeler (one in four are male), but I have elected to go with the statistical odds and present the wife as a Feeler, and the husband as the Thinker.

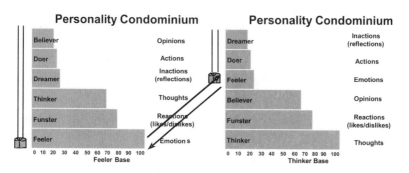

One day the Feeler wife says to her Thinker husband, "I feel so bad." In a perfect world, the husband would have established a Perception connection by going into his elevator, pushing the "Emotion" floor button, getting off at his Feeler floor, and saying something like, "Honey, I love you, and whatever it is, I'm here for you." This is an example of connecting at an Emotions Perception, floor type to floor type. In their marriage, this Thinker has learned how important Emotions are to Feelers, just as this Feeler can learn how important Thoughts are to Thinkers.

When either or both do not appreciate and connect with the other's Perception, the consequences become "communication problems" in the relationship. For example, what if the Thinker had not moved to his Feeler floor, but instead stayed on his Base floor of Thoughts? From a Thoughts-oriented position, Thinkers do not hear "I feel so bad" as a desire to be nurtured, but as an obligation to solve a problem.

Therefore, Thinker husband responds, "How long have you been feeling bad?"

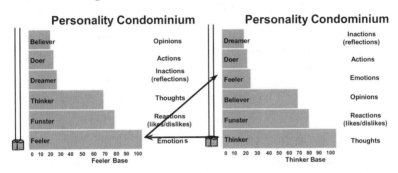

Throughout his life, Thinker husband has found a logical formula to deal with "feeling bad" situations that has served him well for many such "problems."

1. Identify the precipitating event or cause.

2. Initiate a mediating strategy.

3. Have an evaluation procedure for the ongoing intervention.

4. Formulate a prevention plan to anticipate and avoid such future problems.

His "full of thought" question is not really thoughtful of her needs. It requires that she have enough energy to move up to her Thinker floor and activate Thoughts to answer his question. And, it certainly does nothing for her Feeler need to be nurtured.

With an unconscious justification of, "She sure is lucky to have me around to teach her how to think through this," he asks another question: "Was it at one or two o'clock today?"

By now his questions are "felt" as interrogations. Over adaptively she responds with, "I don't know...."

To a Thinker, this only heightens the need for his wife to be taught how to analyze the situation by gathering more facts. However, by this time the lack of evidence of her "thinking" clearly justifies him to push her all the harder, and he moves out of his OK-based condominium into behavior of a distressed Thinker: "Well, was the little hand on the one, or on the two!!!" He is convinced that what has worked so well in his life should work well in the life of the person he loves so much. But he mis-assumes as we all do: "My perception of the world is accurate and is the way you experience the world in order to make it."

We will see in later chapters that in distress, Thinkers experience, "I'm OK–You're not OK because you can't think." And in distress, Feelers experience, "I'm not OK–You're OK, I guess I did something wrong." We are all OK. When we get into distress, it is as if we are wearing a mask. We are still OK, even though the masked behavior is negative.

The Feeler often turns away with, "I wish he would listen to my feelings." The Thinker often turns away thinking, "She has the I.Q. of a begonia. Should I water her?"

Although the context (content) of this miscommunication changes, the resulting bad feelings toward each other continue to build up a wall between them. It all started with not connecting in Perception. How crucial it is to learn, value, and use the other's language.

Each of us speaks all six Perceptual languages, just in varying degrees of fluency. The language of the therapist must match the preferred language of the client in order to ensure connecting and having the content of the interaction "heard."

This requires choosing the Perceptual language, and speaking it to the client. The therapist's personality condominium will determine what languages she is fluent in and which ones need to be practiced. The order of and "bandwidth" (amount of energy) in each floor Perception will reflect this.

A knowledgeable PTM trained therapist knows her own personality structure, and a wise one knows how to use it with each client, second-by-second.

Practice speaking the different Perceptions when you hear someone speak a language other than that of your Base Perception. Listen to how other Personality Types speak their Perceptual language. Can you tell the floor Type he is on by his choice of Perception?

If a person were to use all six of his Personality Type floors to tell the Fairy Tale, "Goldilocks and the Three Bears," it might sound like this:[*]

First floor (Thinker–Thoughts): "Once upon a time there were three bears – a mother bear, a father bear, and a baby bear. I do not know if the baby bear was a male or female, so I think you can make up your own mind to that. Also there was a little girl, called Goldilocks. Perhaps she was called this because of the color of her hair. The facts of the story include her being lost in a forest, all alone. It was night time

---

[*] Since we are often "seduced" by the content into our favorite Perception, a simple, familiar content topic has been selected.

57

and dark. But there was a full moon, which meant that she could see some things. And she did. She saw a cottage. It was about 100 yards away – about the distance of a football field. Because she was tired, it took her almost five minutes to walk to it. When she got there, she knocked three times. She waited for a count of ten, but no one answered. She knocked another three times, and counted to ten, but no one answered."

Second floor (Feeler–Emotions): "Oh the poor little girl – my heart just aches. So alone, and so afraid. I would just love to be able to pick her up and hold her, and say to her, 'Everything is going to be alright, honey.' I feel so sad knowing there are children in this world who are so alone and afraid. But it does my heart good knowing there are caring, giving people who take them in as family and love them as their own."

Third floor (Believer–Opinions): "In my opinion we should not be telling Fairy Tales that contain harmful messages to young, impressionable children. I believe that stories depicting violence, illegal, unethical, or immoral behavior should not be told to children. An account of a witch threatening to bake a little boy and girl should never be considered a topic of discussion with a minor. Parents have an ethical and moral responsibility and should be held accountable for what they tell their children. Parents should not be telling a story about a young lady who breaks into a home and steals food."

Fourth floor (Funster–Reactions (likes/dislikes)): "Wow! Neat beds. Big one, little one, just-my-size one! Oh yes, trampoline time. Starving…need goodies for Goldie. Porridge! I hate porridge. Who lives here? Bears?!"

Fifth floor (Dreamer–Inactions (reflections)): "After a little while Goldilocks became very tired. She reflected about the day, and imagined a far away place where she was safe and secure. In her mind's eye she could see a sunny day, with a lamb grazing leisurely, alone on a hillside. And with those visions, she became more and more tired, and fell restfully and soundly asleep."

Sixth floor (Doer–Actions): "Crash! Through the door bulged three bears. 'Get out of my house!' bellowed the biggest. Startled, and jumping to her feet, Goldilocks defends her position with, 'Chill out bears. Give me a break. Alone and hungry I stumbled to your door. Tell me what you would have done. I break in, I eat. Hey, you saved my life!' 'Let her stay,' pleads the momma bear. 'Make her fix my bed that she broke!,' complains the baby bear. Frowning at the intruder, poppa bear hands Goldilocks a broom, and tells her, 'There ain't no free lunch here – clean up the mess you made.'"

Sometimes we can just start a language, and see if people will speak it. If they do not want to, then their natural language response will alert us to the Perception they prefer. The following examples show the therapist staying in his own Perception, as well as what he could have said in the client's Perception.

Therapist:	**"What option do you think…."** [Thoughts]
Client A:	**"I believe I should…."** [Opinions]
Therapist: [not processing]	**"Then do you think that…. "** [Thoughts]

Therapist: [processing]	"Then in your opinion would...." [Opinions]

Therapist:	"Tell me what you did about it." [Actions]
Client B:	"I would feel so...." [Emotions]
Therapist: [not processing]	"And then do what?" [Actions]
Therapist: [processing]	"Feelings are important...." [Emotions]

Therapist:	"It's OK to share your feelings...." [Emotions]
Client C:	"I thought it was illogical of him...." [Thoughts]
Therapist: [not processing]	"And how did you feel when...." [Emotions]
Therapist: [processing]	"What else were you thinking about him?" [Thoughts]

Therapist:	"In your opinion do you believe she was right?" [Opinions]
Client D:	"What she did was the pits." [Reactions]
Therapist: [not processing]	"Do you believe parents have a responsibility to...." [Opinions]

Therapist: [processing]	"Sounds like you didn't like it." [Reactions]
Therapist:	"Take your time and reflect on your day." [Inactions]
Client E:	"Getting out there and making money is what I need to do." [Actions]
Therapist: [not processing]	"Imagine a peaceful moment in your day and let yourself....' [Inactions]
Therapist: [processing]	"Tell me how you do that." [Actions]
Therapist:	"When I was a kid I hated it when I didn't get my way." [Reactions]
Client F:	"I don't mind. I have a whole world inside of me." [Inactions]
Therapist: [not processing]	"Wow! Sounds like a blast. You really like it there." [Reactions]
Therapist: [processing]	"Imagine you are there, and describe it." [Inactions]

Each of these therapists initially spoke a basic Perceptual language, and probably chose to be trained in a discipline, or from a supervisor, that matched his Perception and Personality Type frame of reference.[*]

Furthermore, each of these therapists working with clients A-F could very well have a valid clinical reason for tracking and inviting the client in the direction his content was suggesting. The point of the above examples was to emphasize the importance of first connecting in Perception, then focusing on content, model, or technique.

Chapter 3. Personality Parts

The other major component in connecting with a client is "Channels." Channels simply are transactions between two people, both of whom are in an OK–OK position on a floor in their personality condominium. A Channel is comprised of an offer from one person and a response from another.[1] Each of these offers and responses is an observable Personality Part of the individual.[2] So in order to understand Channels, we must first identify the Personality Parts.

Dr. Berne posited the existence of what he referred to as "ego states." He defined these as "coherent systems of thought and feeling manifested by corresponding patterns of behavior."[3] These patterns of behavior consisted of the five behavioral cues – words, tones, gestures, postures and facial expressions. I refined transactional theory by identifying the positive and negative parts of these (functional) ego states.

---

[*] Unit 14 identifies famous therapists and how their models are natural projections of their respective Personality Types.

In PTM terminology, the five positive parts that I identified – the "Personality Parts" or the "Parts" – are called: Protector, Director, Computer, Comforter, and Reveler.[4]

The Protector

To be in the Protector part, give a command, imperative, or directive aimed at your own or someone else's senses. For example, "Take a deep breath." "Calm down." "Listen." "Look at me." "Stop." Etc. These are Protector-based provided that no attack, threat or anger is involved.

Words: Any commands that are directed at the five senses (smell, taste, sight, hearing, touch). No threats, attacks, or anger are involved.

Tones: Firm, protective, calm, and accepting.

Gestures: Hands and arms outstretched as if holding and supporting the shoulders of a small child.

Postures: Relaxed, yet stable.

Facial Expressions: Non-critical, open, a slight nod to punctuate that accepting the command is OK; a trustworthy and supportive look.

The Director

To be in the Director, give a command, imperative, or directive aimed at the thinking part of someone. Anger, threats, and attacks are not involved. Examples include: "Tell me what you want to accomplish today." "Respond to her." "Imagine that part of you in

this chair." "Tell me what you were thinking." "Say that to him." All of these are imperatives directed at the other person.

Words: "Tell..." "Say..." "Do..." Any imperative that requires thinking in the other person.

Tones: Firm, non-critical, non-threatening.

Gestures: Few, if any.

Postures: Erect.

Facial Expressions: Neither raised eyebrows nor a frown. Expressionless.

The Computer

The Computer is the asking, fact finding and/or fact giving part of a person. Neither emotions nor opinions are involved. No commands, imperatives, or directives are issued, rather requests are made. Examples include such questions as "What do you want to accomplish?"

"What options do you see?" "Then what happened?"

Words: "What...?" "Will...?" "Is...?" "How...?" Any non-emotional, non-critical fact inquiring question or information giving.

Tones: Monotonic.

Gestures: Few, if any.

Postures: Erect, steady.

Facial Expressions: Expressionless.

The Comforter

To energize your Comforter, assume the qualities of a warm, nurturing parent, addressing the child emotion part of the other person, rather than the Computer thinking part. Examples include, "I really appreciate you." "I understand how much stress you have now, and it's  OK to share your feelings with us." "I'm concerned about you." "You're a warm, sensitive person, and I'm glad you're here." The purpose of the Comforter is not to gain information, but rather to invite someone else to feel nurtured. People who want their feelings acknowledged respond to the Comforter.

Words: "I appreciate you." "You're an important person." "I'm glad you're here." Etc.

Tones: Soft, gentle, soothing, caring, warm.

Gestures: Palms up.

Postures: Relaxed. Open. Extending forward.

Facial Expressions: Accepting, warm, gentle, smiling, soft.

The Reveler

The Reveler is the natural OK feeling part of us. It is not the vengeful, spiteful, teasing or prankster part, but the spontaneous part. Examples include: "Bob, I sure like that tie." (Director might say, "Tell us where you bought that tie."  Nurturer might say, "Bob you have such good taste. I appreciate how you let yourself enjoy your clothes so much.") The Reveler Part says, *"Here'sssssss Mary!"* It is a playful and/or sharing of positive emotions part. No one is put down. A Reveler Part neither laughs at another nor at himself in derogatory ways.

Words: "Wow! You're doing super." "Whew! Fantastic." "I like..." "You've got the tiger by the tail now."

Tones: Up, energetic, enthusiastic, playful, wide range, "rings."

Gestures: Animated, lively.

Postures: Lax, open, fluid, flexible, loose, resilient, elastic.

Facial Expressions: Twinkly, smiles child-like, alive, "natural."

The Reveler also experiences negative, but healthy feelings. Grief, for example, must be experienced with losses. Also, non-blaming anger is expressed from our Reveler Part.

To use a Personality Part, we use the associated behavioral cues. The more cues we use, the more successful we will be. However, as a general rule, we are successful in using the Part when we reflect three of the five cues.

Just as each Personality Type has a language to show the underlying Perception, so does each Personality Type have a Part that it uses to communicate.

Floor Type	Character Strengths	Perception	Part
Thinker	Responsible, logical, organized	Thoughts	Computer
Feeler	Compassionate, sensitive, warm	Emotions	Comforter
Believer	Dedicated, observant, conscientious	Opinions	Computer
Funster	Spontaneous, creative, playful	Reactions (likes/dislikes)	Reveler
Doer	Adaptable, persuasive, charming	Actions	Director
Dreamer	Calm, imaginative, reflective	Inactions (reflections)	Computer

To access and use one of these Parts, we must move to the personality floor within us that "houses" that Part, just as we would to experience the world through a particular Perception. Just as we can measure the energy that is available in each of our six Personality Types, so can we measure the availability of each of the four Parts other than the Protector.

Note in the chart above that the Computer Part is used by three Personality Types: Thinker, Believer, and Dreamer. They use the Computer in different ways. The Thinker uses the Computer to get, organize, and give information. The Believer uses the Computer to support and offer values. The Dreamer uses the Computer to be imaginative and introspective. A PTM trained therapist can use her knowledge of Personality Types to know which Parts the client will show more often. Also, by observing the Parts that a client uses most, the therapist will obtain useful information about the client's personality structure.

Chapter Notes

[1] Kahler, Taibi. *Managing with the Process Communication Model,* Human Development Publications, Little Rock, 1979.
[2] *Ibid.*
[3] Berne, Eric. *Games People Play,* Grove Press, New York, 1964.
[4] See *Op. Cit.* at 1.

Chapter 4. Channels

When people communicate effectively, they will be in one of five "Channels." Just as a short wave radio or walkie talkie requires both parties to be on the same frequency in order that each be heard, so does communication require that individuals be on the same Channel in everyday life in order for information to be heard clearly.

In PTM, we have developed a Rule of Communication. This rule is:

**Communication will take place
if there is an offer and acceptance
in the same Channel.**[1]

What are offers and acceptances in this context? They are the use of the specific Personality Parts that are associated with the Channel. The "offer" is the use of the initial Personality Part in an interaction. "Acceptance" means a crisp response using the correct Personality Part for the Channel offered. From now on, when we say "communicate" we mean the Rule of Communication was followed.

There are five Channels presented, each with a Personality Part offer and a Personality Part acceptance.[2] Since each Part has been identified with mutually exclusive words, tones, gestures, postures, and facial expressions, it is possible to determine interaction-by-interaction whether the therapist and client are communicating or miscommunicating. If the Personality Part of a given Channel is offered by the therapist and the client accepts the offer by responding with the other associated Personality Part, then there has been communication. Any other response indicates a level of miscommunication and most often the beginnings of distress.

These five Channels are called: Intervening, Directing, Asking, Comforting, and Playing.[3]

Intervening Channel

The Intervening Channel "interrupts" one of the three degrees of miscommunication outlined later. The offer comes from the Protector Part with directives, imperatives, or commands aimed at the senses (touch, smell, taste, hearing, or sight) of another or of self. The acceptance is from the Sensor Part of the other person, or that part of one's personality that experiences the basic senses. The Sensor Part's response is non-verbal.

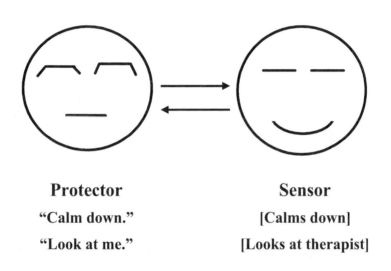

Protector	**Sensor**
"Calm down."	[Calms down]
"Look at me."	[Looks at therapist]

Directing Channel

The Directing Channel offers the Director Part of our personality and invites acceptance from the Computer Part of us.

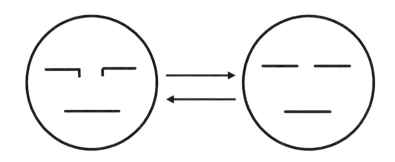

Director	Computer
"Tell me your sleeping patterns."	**"I don't fall asleep until morning."**
"Say more about that."	**"I keep thinking of all that I have to do."**
"Pick one that you often think of."	**"I have to be responsible."**
"Tell me about the first time you can remember having to be responsible."	**"I was ten years old."**
"Be ten. Tell me what's happening."	**"I'm ten, and Mom's sick. Dad's been dead for two years and we don't have any money."**

To be in a Director Personality Part, one gives a command, an imperative, or a directive aimed at somebody else's Computer (thinking part).

This Director Part does not indicate a position of superiority. Instead, it tells somebody what to do and requires thinking to do it. In the Directing Channel, one person offers a command, imperative, or directive and the other person accepts this offer, by responding crisply as a computer would in taking the command (responding with either the requested information or action), without feeling put upon or put down. Note that with this Channel, the directive could be to perform an action, such as "get the papers" and the response could be the performance of the directed action.

Asking Channel

The Asking Channel involves the exchange of thoughts or opinions from Computer to Computer.

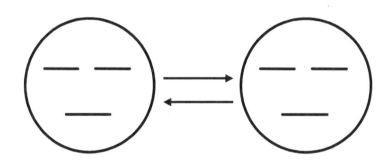

Computer	**Computer**
"What are your sleeping patterns?"	"I don't fall asleep until morning."
"Why?"	"I keep thinking of all that I have to do."
"Why is that important?"	"I have to be responsible."

"Do you remember one of the first times that you had to be responsible?"	"Yes, I was ten years old."
"Will you imagine that you are ten again, and will you tell me what's happening as if I were there with you?"	"I'm ten, and Mom's sick. Dad's been dead for two years and we don't have any money"

The Asking Channel of communication consists of the exchange of clear, crisp, information. Feelings are not involved and questions are answered directly, like two computers exchanging data.

Comforting Channel

This Channel has an offer from the Comforter Part of us – the warm, nurturing, caring, sensitive parent. The complementary acceptance is from the Reveler Part – the authentic natural feeling Part. The Comforter Channel is not aimed at exchanging ideas, but rather at inviting someone else to feel cared for.

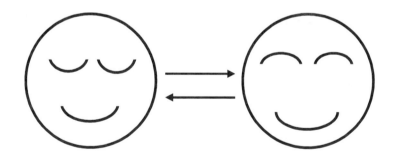

Comforter	**Reveler**
"Jim, I appreciate you saying how you are feeling."	"You're welcome."

"Mary, it's ok to share your feelings here."

"Thank you."

"Thanks for being you."

"Wow."

Playing Channel

This Channel is like two kids being playful with one another.

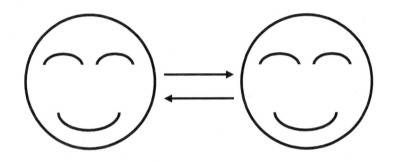

Reveler

Reveler

"Chu look mahvlous."

"And I feel mahvlous."

"I like working with you."

"I like working with you too."

"Yikes, it's hot!"

"By golly, it sure is!"

"I'll take even a lukewarm fuzzy any day."

"And I'll pass on a chilly prickly any day."

This Channel of communication is an energizing exchange from the playful Parts of each person. This playful, *non-teasing*, exchange helps people be "up" and excited, and creates a non-threatening fun, child-like atmosphere.

When we move our energy to a given floor of our personality condominium, we can access all the behaviors associated with that floor's Personality Type. So, when desiring the use of the character strengths of being spontaneous, creative, and playful, then moving to the Funster floor is required. When desiring the use of the Perception of Emotions, then moving to the Feeler floor is required. When desiring the use of a Director Part, then moving to the Doer floor is required. When desiring the use of the Asking Channel, then moving to the Thinker or Believer floor is required, depending on the Perception.

Floor Type	Channel	Part to Part
Thinker	Asking:	Computer to Computer
Feeler	Comforting:	Comforter to Reveler
Believer	Asking:	Computer to Computer
Funster	Playing:	Reveler to Reveler
Doer	Directing:	Director to Computer
Dreamer (receives)	Directing:	Director to Computer

This table identifies the Personality Type floor and the Channel housed there.[*]

Note that the Dreamer uses the Computer Part to receive the Directing Channel. However, unlike the other Personality Types, no Channel is initiated from the Dreamer floor. Rather, a person with a Dreamer Base who initiates moves to a different floor of his or her personality to do so.

If the above diagram reflected the personality condominium of a client in order, with Dreamer as the Base and Thinker as the sixth floor, then the therapist would use most often the Directing Channel, and least often the Asking

---

[*] From original 1972 Research data.

and Comforting Channels, especially if the PTMP scores for these Channels were less than 20.

Chapter Notes

[1] Kahler, Taibi. *Managing with the Process Communication Model,* Kahler Communications, Inc. Little Rock, 1982.
[2] *Ibid.*
[3] *Ibid.*

Chapter 5: Channels and Perceptions

Connecting with a client most effectively combines using both the client's favorite Channel and her favorite Perception, each of which is associated with the client's Base Personality Type.

Doer floor: Directing Channel + Actions

The Doer floor houses the Directing Channel and Actions.

Directing Channel

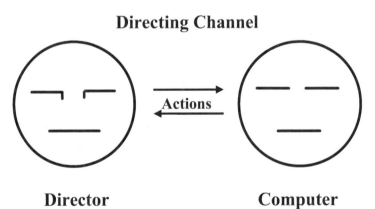

Director	Computer
"Tell her what you're going to do."	"I'm going to take you dancing once a month."

"Say to each person what you are going to do when given a compliment."

"When I am given a compliment, I will say 'Thank you'."

Thinker floor: Asking Channel + Thoughts

The Thinker floor houses the Asking Channel and Thoughts.

Asking Channel

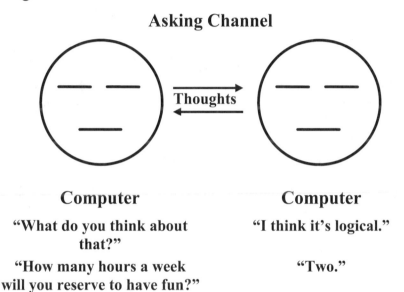

Computer

"What do you think about that?"

"How many hours a week will you reserve to have fun?"

Computer

"I think it's logical."

"Two."

Believer floor: Asking Channel + Opinions

The Believer floor houses the Asking Channel and Opinions.

Asking Channel

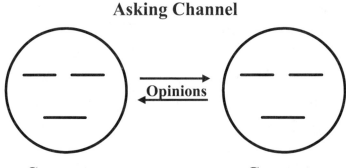

Computer

"What's your opinion about that?"

"When do you believe you should resume your sessions?"

Computer

"I believe it will be valuable."

"I believe I should start coming on Wednesdays."

Feeler floor: Comforting Channel + Emotions

The Feeler floor houses the Comforting Channel and Emotions.

Comforting Channel

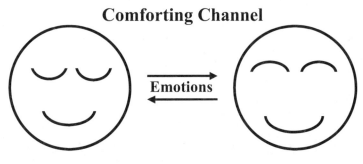

Comforter

"It's OK to say what you feel."

"Thank you for sharing your feelings with the group."

Reveler

"I feel so sad."

"You're welcome. I feel better."

Funster floor: Playing Channel + Reactions
(likes/dislikes)

The Funster floor houses the Playing Channel and Reactions.

Playing Channel

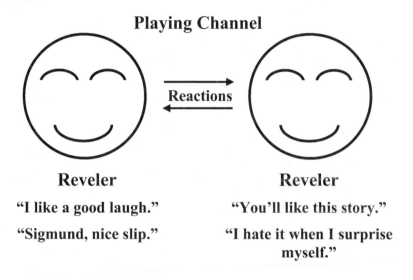

Reveler	Reveler
"I like a good laugh."	"You'll like this story."
"Sigmund, nice slip."	"I hate it when I surprise myself."

Dreamer floor: Directive Channel + Inactions
(reflections)

Dreamers respond to Directive Channel and Inactions but must move to another floor to initiate.

Directing Channel

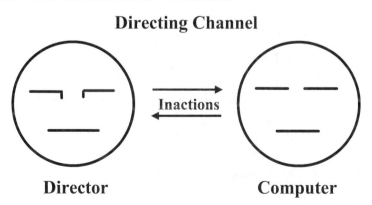

Director   Computer

| "Imagine your Father with a smile, not a frown." | "I can see him." |
| "Reflect on a time and place where you were safe and secure." | "I'm there." |

The following diagram identifies the Personality Type floor and the Channel and Perception housed there.

Floor Type	Channel	Perception
Feeler	Comforting	Emotions
Funster	Playing	Reactions (likes/dislikes)
Doer	Directing	Actions
Dreamer (receives)	Directing	Inactions (reflections)
Thinker	Asking	Thoughts
Believer	Asking	Opinions

If the above diagram reflected the personality condominium of a client in order, with Believer as the Base first floor and Feeler as the sixth floor, then the therapist would use most often the Asking Channel with Opinions and Thoughts (respectively), and least often the Comforting Channel or Emotions, especially if the PTMP scores for these Channels were less than 20. If the Funster floor score was also low, then the therapist would be wise to avoid playfulness or humor.

The following personality condominium indicates that the therapist is most likely to make a connection with this person by asking questions aimed at eliciting facts: using the Asking Channel with Thoughts. Funster, Feeler, and Believer floors are also "open," as the scores for those Personality Types exceed 40. Using the Directing Channel aimed at Reflections or Actions would prove unproductive.

Personality Condominium

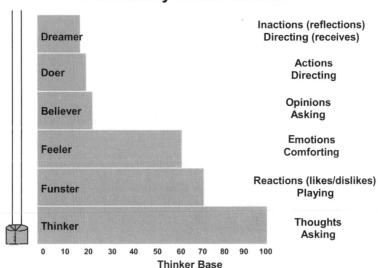

Unit Three
Drivers: First Degree Distress

In the late 1960's I discovered a sequence of distress that was identifiable by observing the behavioral cues, starting with Drivers (defense-like behaviors lasting only a few seconds). Subsequent research resulted in the identification of a unique Driver for each Personality Type. I sometimes describe the Drivers as the doorway to distress.

Chapter 1. "Doc, I Can't Take this Floor Anymore"

As we have seen, each person has a personality structure made up of all six Personality Types. The strongest of these is at the base of the structure and the others layer on top of it in decreasing order of strength. The strength of each Personality Type in a structure dictates how much energy, or "bandwidth," the person has to experience the world using that floor of their personality. Thus, when a client is invited to move her energies to a Personality Type floor by either a Channel offer or the use of a Perceptual language, there is just a given amount of bandwidth she has to stay in that floor and communicate. That's why the therapist is wise to connect at the client's Base, first floor. When the therapist does not monitor process, but rather projects her own favored Channel and Perception, then connecting with the client becomes problematic.

Each Base Personality Type has a "doorway" leading out of the condominium of OK'ness into distress. This doorway is called a Driver.[1] It functions as an observable defense mechanism indicating that the individual is experiencing the onset of distress. A Driver lasts only a second or two, is not associated with a feeling, but does reflect a behavioral life position of "OK if..." The Driver is the first of the three degrees of distress – First Degree Distress.

The process value to the therapist in identifying and understanding Drivers is simple, yet profound: when a therapist uses a Channel or Perception that the client cannot energize and respond to, then the client will, instead, show the Driver behavior of his Base Personality Type.

Drivers, then, have great process information value. They alert the therapist: 1) to whether or not he is using the correct Channel and Perception to connect with the client; and 2) to the Channel and Perception that should be used next.

Since the Driver functions as a yellow light from the Base cautioning the therapist not to continue using the previous Channel or Perception, it is at the same time signaling to the therapist to use the Channel and Perception of the Base instead.

The appearance of the Driver in an interaction signals that miscommunication is beginning. When we see or hear a person's Driver, we are inclined to respond with our own Driver. This can lead to ever decreasing communication, to clouded thinking and, in some cases, to the start of a Distress Sequence in one or both of the parties to the interaction.

Chapter 2. The Base Thinker Driver: "I Must Be Perfect"

The Thinker First Degree Distress Be perfect (for you) Driver reflects a behavioral life position of, "I must be perfect to be OK–You're OK."[1]

Words	Tones	Gestures	Postures	Facial Expressions
unneeded qualifications: "to me, personally"	measured	punctuating with fingers or the hand	measured, robot like	strained

Although all five behavioral cues of words, tones, gestures, postures, and facial expressions must confirm a Driver, the simplest way to recognize this Driver is when a person makes an over-qualifying statement. For example, "I'm not exactly sure what you mean." Without distress this could be expressed by the Computer, "What do you mean?"

Or, "I don't know if by 'feeling' you mean emotional, psychological, or physical." Without distress this could be expressed by the Computer, "What do you mean by 'feeling'?"

Or, "Right now, this second, I'm feeling, within myself, some measure of sadness." Without distress this could be expressed by the Reveler, "I'm sad."

So when a therapist offers a Channel or Perception aimed at a personality floor seldom visited by a Thinker Base client, the client will likely respond with a Be perfect (for you) Driver.

Consider the following personality condominium structure of a client:

Personality Condominium

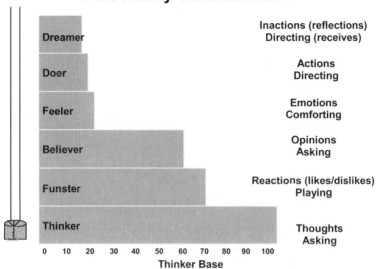

Dreamer	Inactions (reflections) Directing (receives)
Doer	Actions Directing
Feeler	Emotions Comforting
Believer	Opinions Asking
Funster	Reactions (likes/dislikes) Playing
Thinker	Thoughts Asking

0 10 20 30 40 50 60 70 80 90 100
Thinker Base

If the therapist gives many imperatives (Directing Channel), or focuses on having this Thinker Base client express emotions, the result from the client is likely to be a Be perfect Driver because the client runs out of energy trying to be on his three weakest floors. Again, this is the natural defense of the client, not defensiveness.

The gift the client is giving to the therapist is: "How you are attempting to help me may have benefited you or may be how you were taught to do therapy, but it does not fit my structure. My Be perfect Driver will advertise that you can connect with me if you will first use more Thoughts and logic, and ask me questions, instead of giving me imperatives."

Therapist (again):   "So, tell me how you feel about that."

Client [Be perfect]:   "I'm not exactly sure what you mean by 'feel about it.'"

85

Therapist:	"Say what you're feeling."
Client [Be perfect]:	"Right now, inside, I'm not 100 percent sure."

The therapist who monitors process would be alerted to the initial Thinker Be perfect Driver, shift to her own Thinker floor, and use an Asking Channel aimed at Thoughts. The therapist shifts her floor to the client's to invite him out of First Degree Distress by offering that which is most familiar within his personality structure - Thinker Base.

Process Therapist:	"What are you experiencing?"

(This is in the Asking Channel and allows the client first to "think" about the emotion).

Client:	"I have a tightening in my throat and a tear on my cheek."

(The client is out of the Driver and in the OK-OK condominium.)

Chapter Notes

[1] Kahler, Taibi. *Process Therapy in Brief,* Human Development Publications, Little Rock, 1979.

Chapter 3. The Base Believer Driver: "You Must Be Perfect"

The Believer First Degree Distress Be perfect (for me) Driver[*] reflects a behavioral life position of "I'm OK– You're OK as long as you're perfect." [1]

---

[*] This Driver is often written, "Be perfect-P," to indicate the "parent" position of "I'm OK."

Words	Tones	Gestures	Postures	Facial Expressions
big words when little would do	precise	calculated	rigid	head cocked up
over qualifying			stiff	piercing eyes
over detailing			aloof	
over questioning				

The simplest way to recognize this Driver is when a person asks an over-qualifying question. For example, "What exactly do you mean?" Without distress this could be expressed by the Computer, "What do you mean?" Note that this differs from the Thinker Be perfect (for you) Driver, which is evidenced by an over-qualifying *statement.*

Or, "When precisely will you arrive?" Without distress this could be expressed by the Computer, "When will you be there?"

Or, "Right now, this second, what are you feeling, within yourself?" Without distress this could be expressed by the Computer, "What are you feeling?"

So when a therapist offers a Channel or Perception aimed at a personality floor seldom visited by a Believer Base client, the client will likely respond with a Be perfect (for me) Driver.

Consider the following personality condominium structure of a client:

Personality Condominium

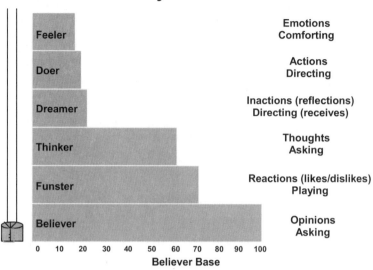

	Emotions Comforting
Feeler	
	Actions Directing
Doer	
	Inactions (reflections) Directing (receives)
Dreamer	
	Thoughts Asking
Thinker	
	Reactions (likes/dislikes) Playing
Funster	
	Opinions Asking
Believer	

0 10 20 30 40 50 60 70 80 90 100

Believer Base

What if a Feeler trained therapist stayed in his Base floor with a Comforting Channel and Perceptual language of Emotions?

Therapist: "I just want you to feel totally at ease with me. I genuinely care about my clients, and unconditionally accept what you tell me, and who you are. It's OK to share whatever you're feeling with me and be open."

Client [Be perfect-P]: "What exactly do you mean by 'open'?"

Therapist: "It's OK to say whatever you're feeling."

Client [Be perfect-P]: "What if I don't know precisely what I'm feeling?"

Therapist: "That's OK too. Just be you."

Client

[Be perfect-P]: "Are you aware that 'Just be you," even though preceded by your claim of genuine care for all, has a denigratory connotation?"

It is painfully clear that this therapist and client are not connecting. It would be interesting to hear what the therapist "felt" was happening and why it happened.

A Process Therapist would have recognized the "What exactly do you mean by 'open'?" as a Be perfect (for me) Driver, and he would have realized that the next intervention needed to be aimed at the Believer floor with a Perception of Opinions and an Asking Channel.

For example, "Ah, I too believe it's important to define terms. In my opinion, 'open' means trust. And I believe trust is something that must be earned. So, we need to earn each other's trust. Trust should be based on being reliable. Reliability is making agreements and keeping them. I am willing to make and keep contracts with you. If you believe that could be valuable for us, then in your opinion, what should we agree to?"

Chapter Notes

[1] Kahler, Taibi. *Process Therapy in Brief,* Human Development Publications, Little Rock, 1979.

Chapter 4. The Base Feeler Driver: "I Must Please"

The Feeler First Degree Distress Please you Driver reflects a behavioral life position of, "I'm OK as long as I Please you–You're OK."[1]

Words	Tones	Gestures	Postures	Facial Expressions
"maybe"	whine	head nodding with chin tucked	shoulders in	raised eyebrows
"kinda"	raises at the end of sentence		head forward	mousy
"you know"				looking up

The simplest way to recognize this Driver is when a person over adapts, often with raised tone and eyebrows. An example is, "Maybe you could say that again." Without distress this could be expressed by the Computer, "Will you say that again?"

When a therapist does not talk enough emotion Perception language or offer the Nurturing Channel, but rather speaks in Perceptions or Channels of floors not often visited by the Feeler client, then the result is a Please you Driver.

Personality Condominium

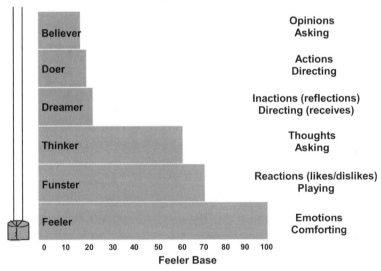

Consider the foregoing personality condominium structure of a Feeler client: Let's say the therapist has a Believer Base and a Feeler floor that he seldom visits. Then he will offer Opinions as his strongest natural Perception using the Asking Channel. Values and beliefs will be a natural therapeutic frame of reference for this therapist.

Therapist:	"What do you believe would be valuable to work on today?"
Client [Please you]:	"Maybe you could suggest what I should work on."
Therapist:	"I believe it is important for you to distinguish between rational and irrational opinions about things in your life. You said your neighbor was spying on you. Why do you believe that?"
Client [Please you]:	"You mean the one next door."
Therapist:	"Do you believe anyone is spying on you?"
Client [Please you]:	"You mean John."

The Client's responses with raised tones are Please you Drivers, not questions in Asking Channel. She does not have the energy to move to her Believer floor and respond to Opinions in the Asking Channel.

Remember the Feeler therapist who did not connect with the Believer client? That therapist would have connected with this client with "I just want you to feel totally at ease with me..." because this approach matches this client's Feeler Base and openness to Emotions and a Comforting Channel.

Chapter Notes

[1.] Kahler, Taibi. *Process Therapy in Brief,* Human Development Publications, Little Rock, 1979.

Chapter 5. The Base Funster Driver: "I Must Try Hard"

The Funster First Degree Distress Try Hard Driver reflects a behavioral life position of "I'm OK as long as I Try hard for you–You're OK."[1]

Words	Tones	Gestures	Postures	Facial Expressions
"I can't"	strained	helpless	leaning forward, bent down, head up	struggling
"ah..."				
not asking directly	pressured			wrinkled
"I don't know"				

A person is in a Try hard Driver when she invites the other person to think for her by seeming not to understand. For example, "I don't understand." This is a Try hard Driver because there is an implied "do something for me" and no real request.

Had the person really not understood and wanted to understand, then there would have been a Channel. For example, "I don't understand. Will you explain that?"

As we have discovered with each of these Base Personality Type Drivers, they are advertisements for two things: 1) "I no longer have energy to respond to your Perception and/or Channel offers," and 2) "If you want to communicate with me, then use the Perception and/or

92

Channel that matches the Driver Personality Type that I just showed you."

Consider the following personality condominium of a client:

Personality Condominium

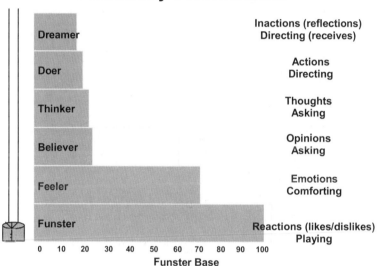

Let's say the therapist has a Thinker Base and naturally uses the Asking Channel with the Perception of Thoughts.

Therapist: "Did you think about what we discussed last week?"

Client [Try hard]: "I don't remember."

Therapist: "We talked about your taking responsibility for mistakes that you have made."

Client [Try hard]: "Mistakes...Like...ah...ah..."

Therapist:	"You identified three mistakes, and said you would not blame anyone if you made those mistakes again. Do you remember them?"

Client [Try hard]:	"I'm not following you ... not blame..."

This dance could go on for the entire session. The Process Therapist would have responded to the first Try hard Driver, realizing that the client was not in Channel, neither in response nor offer.

For example, the Process Therapist could have responded to the Try hard "I don't remember," with the Perception of Reactions in the Playing Channel: "I sure don't like it when I can't remember. I'll give you a hint – an unmarried New York strip, and not Mr. Steak, or Mrs. Steak."

The Try hard Driver of the Funster is often difficult for Thinkers and Believers because they are so concrete oriented that they assume the Driver is content, not process based.

An "I don't understand" is interpreted as "Do you have information for me?" But that is not what the Driver advertises. To the contrary, the First Degree Distressed Funster is saying just the opposite: "If you keep giving me your thoughts/opinions, I'll keep Trying hard and avoid taking responsibility for myself."

Here's a simple test. The next time a Funster offers you in real life a Try hard Driver of "I don't understand" or "I don't get it," and you respond with an Asking Channel aimed at Thoughts, with "What is it you do not understand?" or "What is it that you don't get?" don't expect a Channel response. You're not likely to get one. Instead you may end up frustrated after a few exchanges.

The payoff for a distressed Funster is to see Thinkers and Believers frustrated.

For example, in Chapter 7 of the Introduction, I identified the game of "Why Don't You, Yes But." The initiator gives a Try hard Con of, "I've got a problem. My garage door sticks." To avoid the payoff of frustration, a Thinker or Believer could have stopped playing the game at the Gimmick by dealing with the Try hard driver with the Playing Channel plus Reactions: "I hate it when my garage door sticks, too."[*]

Chapter Notes

[1.] Kahler, Taibi. *Process Therapy in Brief,* Human Development Publications, Little Rock, 1979.

Chapter 6. The Base Dreamer Driver: "I Must Be Strong"

The Dreamer First Degree Distress Be strong (for you) Driver reflects a behavioral life position of "I'm OK as long as I Be strong for you–You're OK."[1]

---

[*] It is interesting to note that Dr. Berne's antithesis to this game is, "That is a problem. What are you going to do about it?" This appears to put responsibility back onto the initiator, but since it is delivered in the Asking Channel with Thoughts, it is not likely to be totally effective. Dr. Berne was likely a Believer in a Thinker Phase.

Words	Tones	Gestures	Postures	Facial Expressions
"it came to me"	monotonic	(none)	rigid	molded
"it occurred to me"			frozen	cold
"that makes me feel"				expressionless

The easy way to recognize this Driver is when a person implies that someone or something is in charge of his thoughts or feelings. For example, "It came to me," rather than "I thought of it." Or, "It hurts," rather than "I hurt."

When a therapist does not use enough Directing Channel and/or Inactions (reflections), then the result is a Be strong from the client.

Consider a Base Thinker therapist, who naturally uses the Asking Channel with Thoughts, working with a client who has little Thinker energy (it is her sixth floor).

Therapist: "I think contracts are useful. First you think of what you want to change, then you put it into measurable terms, then you decide what you think is an attainable goal, and then you put that into measurable terms. And finally you and I agree you will accomplish this. So, what do you think you want to change?"

Client [Be strong]: "Nothing occurs to me."

Therapist: "I think a logical way to proceed is to think about change on a scale from one to ten. One is considered to be very unimportant. Ten is to be considered very important. So if you were to think of one concern of yours that you would score above a seven, what would it be?"

Client [Be strong]: "That doesn't make sense."

Therapist: "What doesn't make sense?"

Client [Be strong]: "It doesn't make sense."

Therapist: "How do you define 'it'?"

Client [Be strong]: "Nothing comes to me."

And around we go. Or, in the world of the Dreamer in First Degree Distress Be strong Driver, "around it goes."

The Process Therapist would have picked up on the first Be strong response of, "Nothing occurs to me." Then she would have processed with a Dreamer floor Directing Channel and encouraged into actions (reflections) in order to invite the client out of First Degree Distress. For example, "Reflect for a moment, and tell me what you want to do differently."

Chapter Notes

[1] Kahler, Taibi. *Process Therapy in Brief,* Human Development Publications, Little Rock, 1979.

Chapter 7. The Base Doer Driver: "You Must Be Strong"

The Doer First Degree Distress Be strong (for me) Driver reflects a behavioral life position of "I'm OK-You're OK as long as you are strong for me."[1]

Words	Tones	Gestures	Postures	Facial Expressions
"What made you think...?"	meant to impress	exaggerated	imposing	confident
"you" for "I"				few eye blinks
"How did he make you feel?"				

Doer Base clients want bottom line results that are action oriented, couched in excitement and drama. Action and the Directing Channel are the connecting secrets, while other Channels and Perceptions that are on the higher floors are often ignored by the Doer client.

Let's take a Funster with Player Channel and Reactions (likes/dislikes) for the therapist.

Therapist: "Oh, the crossed legs and arms and frown from ear to ear. Someone didn't like this week."

Client [Be strong-P]: "You do what you have to do. Your family has to follow your lead. I wasn't given a silver platter, and there ain't no free lunch. Get the picture if you're a kid of mine."

Therapist: "Two chair time. In this chair you like it when your kid follows you. In this one you like it when he is independent."

Client [Be strong-P]: "You pay an arm and a leg to see a therapist. You don't want to play musical chairs."

A Process Therapist would have recognized the Be strong-P of "You do what you have to do," and responded with a Directing Channel with Actions to invite the client out of First Degree Distress. For example, "Tell me what you do with your son." *

The use of Gestalt techniques, including two chair work, may be beneficial with this client. However, deal with the process first, then choose a technique.

Chapter Notes

[1] Kahler, Taibi. *Process Therapy in Brief,* Human Development Publications, Little Rock, 1979.

Chapter 8. Transference or Counter Transference?

We can conclude that all transactions are projections, through choice of Channel and Perception. Truly "working with the client" means understanding the client's personality structure and moving into her frame of reference, interaction by interaction, with Channel and Perception.

Since Drivers are the doorway into distress, the risk the therapist runs by staying in a frame of reference of his own favorite Channel and Perception is to invite the client further into distress. Would this constitute process counter transference?

---

* Another way in which the Doer client might show his Driver is by implying that someone is not in charge his own thoughts or feelings – "How did he (that) make you feel?" Note that this is different than the Driver of the Dreamer. The Dreamer's Driver is self-referential, while the Doer's is directed at another.

Certainly, if focusing on process before content is crucial, it explains why no one "technique or model" fits all clients.

Chapter 9. Assessing with Drivers

Most people demonstrate Base Driver behavior thousands of times a day, indicating this minor level of distress.[*] Therefore to the diagnostician, knowing the six Driver behaviors is a reliable and rapid means of Base assessment. By combining this with listening for Perception, and testing with Channel, the astute observer can determine a person's Base Personality Type within seconds, and verify within minutes.

Base Type	Perception	Channel	Driver
Thinker	Thoughts	Asking	Be perfect
Believer	Opinions	Asking	Be perfect-P
Feeler	Emotions	Comforting	Please you
Doer	Actions	Directing	Be strong-P
Funster	Reactions (likes/dislikes)	Playing	Try hard
Dreamer	Inactions (reflections)	Directing	Be strong

---

[*] To some, this may seem hard to believe. For every minute of verbal interaction, however, it is common for the Driver to be presented 6 to 8 times, each lasting no more than a second or two. These Driver behaviors are interspersed among the instances of good, clear communication.

Chapter 10. Confronting Drivers

Avoid pointing out Drivers: instead "confront" them by using the appropriate Channel and/or Perception to invite the person out of distress and back into the condominium. I originally considered "permissions" to stop the Drivers to be therapeutic but found them to be inappropriate.

The Driver may be associated unconsciously with an early, fantasized consequence, and therefore is serving as a defense mechanism. For example, "If I don't please you, you will reject me." Identifying this Driver, or encouraging the person to stop it, is counter productive. Instead, dealing with the "impasse" is the therapeutic goal.[*]

Since Drivers act as emotional Geiger counters, the purpose is not to get rid of them, but to utilize them.

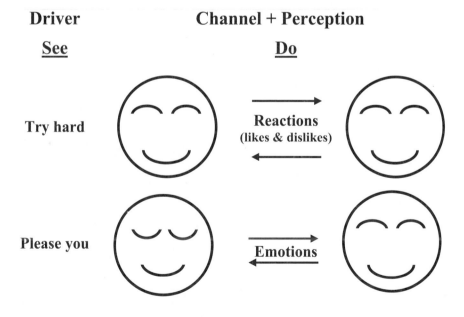

Driver	Channel + Perception
See	Do

Try hard — Reactions (likes & dislikes)

Please you — Emotions

---

[*] This will be covered in detail in later chapters.

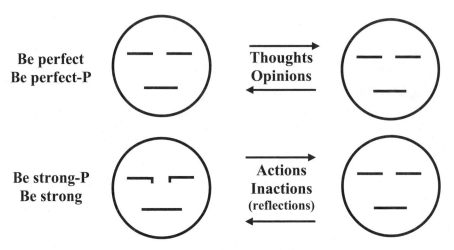

Be perfect
Be perfect-P

Thoughts
Opinions

Be strong-P
Be strong

Actions
Inactions
(reflections)

It has been my experience that by using this simple technique, a therapist will be successful in inviting the client out of First Degree Distress over 80% of the time.

Unit Four
Scripts

Dr. Berne was fascinated with legend and heroes, and studied Greek mythology. In his book, <u>Sex in Human Loving</u>, he defined a script as a blueprint for life, and identified six of them.[1] PTM research showed how these scripts and others are manifested and reinforced. In this Unit, I provide some background on that research and the conclusions reached from it. Detailed material on scripts appears in later Units.

Chapter 1. Berne's Scripts

In this 1970 book, Dr. Berne identified six life scripts: Never, Always, Until, After, Over and Over, and Open Ended.[2] He gave a thesis and a mythological explanation for each. He did not, however, integrate them with ego states, transactions, roles, Distress Sequences, games, personality typology or clinical adaptations. Some of the original Transactional Analysis ("TA") theorists postulated that the script was a result of script injunctions. However, no one had researched scripts to find correlations to help determine causalities.

Chapter Notes

[1] Berne, Eric. *Sex in Human Loving,* Simon and Schuster, New York, 1970.
[2] *Ibid.*

Chapter 2. Drivers and Scripts

I had inserted life script items into my 1972 Research study and found stronger correlations between Drivers and scripts than between injunctions and scripts. This was inconsistent with the postulations of the early script theorists. They believed the script to be the result of injunctions, but there was no research, only theory.

In 1966, Claude Steiner coined the TA term injunction, referring to a negative message that prohibits or inhibits the free behavior of the child.[1] I believe this was a brilliant insight into the structural dynamics of parental distressed behavior.

As I attempted to interpret my research results during the summer of 1971, I asked myself a simple question: "What is it, that is to say, that occurs hundreds of times a day that could reinforce a life script." I smiled, realizing that I had "committed" a Be Perfect Driver with the parenthetical, "that is to say." And Eureka! I had the answer! As a person moves into Drivers, energy is drained from the Adult, and this affects how we pre-consciously structure our thoughts, as evidenced by Driver contaminated sentence patterns. Within hours, I hypothesized the sentence patterns of the scripts and verified the significance of the Driver – script combinations in the research data.[2]

The following diagram identifies the process scripts that PTM research has shown are directly correlated to individual Personality Types and, in two cases, specific combinations of Base Personality and Phase Personality (the "Scripts").

Failure Pattern	Sentence Pattern	Example
Until	—— ( ) ——→	"I can't use, or even attempt to implement, this until I know it perfectly."
Never	(zigzag arrows pattern)	"A thought occurred to me that Workaholics…, Drivers and Scripts seem…, Failure Mechanisms bother me because…"
After	—— but —— (with curved arrow)	"You know I really liked all the people and the material, but I just know I'll forget everything by tomorrow."
Always	✕ — ✕ ——→	"If I start to use this material I'll probably mess up, but if I don't try it I've wasted my time reading this book."
Almost I	+ + + + + —	"I understand Personality Types and Parts, Channels, Psychological Needs, Contact Perceptions and Failure Mechanisms; but I just don't get Drivers."
Almost II	——————— / ↗	"I understand that process is…I hope I'll remember to use what I've learned."

Chapter Notes

[1] Steiner, Claude. "Scripts and Counterscripts," *Transactional Analysis Bulletin,* 1966.
[2] Kahler, Taibi. "Personality Pattern Inventory Validation Studies," Kahler Communications, Inc., 1982.

Chapter 3. Scripts: Process and Content

Further empirical observations, as well as my 1982 research, verified my Script findings.[1] I published them in articles and books, beginning with the miniscript in 1974.[2] In the 1975 article, "Scripts: Process and Content," I integrated both Drivers and script injunction theories into the development of life scripts.[3] I point out that Drivers (functional counterscripts) cause the script by altering sentence patterns. These altered sentence patterns reinforce subtly, yet hundreds of times a day, the script theses. So "counterscript Drivers" cause the formation of the life script. However, injunctions (at Second Degree Distress) determine how intensely – to what degree of harm – we will play out the script.

In another 1975 article called "Drivers: The Key to the Process of Scripts," I gave the correlations between Drivers and sentence patterns and life scripts.[4]

Knowing a client's Script is invaluable. Just as this model was able to predict astronauts' potential Script failure patterns when in distress, it can predict for a therapist how the client might sabotage herself in therapy or in her life.

After analyzing the results of the 1982 research data, I realized that although Base Personality Types had a certain Script because of the correlation, Phasing created new miniscripts, and therefore a new Script.[5] This required analyzing the data, looking at the ordering of six Personality Types within an individual, and then looking at the script for a given Phase Personality within that structure: 4,320 combinations.

Therefore, some of the original information that I published in my 1978 book, *Transactional Analysis Revisited*, was not complete.[6] The data shows that while a given Personality Type or adaptation will have a given Script, that Script can change if a person Phases (as has two-thirds of the population). Also, the new Script might not be the one associated with the new Phase Personality. Rather, it could be a Script that is specific to the Base Personality/Phase Personality combination. For example, a Thinker in a Feeler Phase will not have the "After" Script as his Phase Script (the one correlated with the Feeler Personality Type). Instead, he will have an "Almost II" Script and experience "Is this all there is?" when in distress.

Chapter Notes

[1] Kahler, Taibi. "Personality Pattern Inventory Validation Studies," Kahler Communications, Inc., 1982.

[2] Kahler, Taibi with Hedges Capers. "The Miniscript," *TA Journal,* Jan. 1974.

[3] Kahler, Taibi. "Scripts: Content and Process," *TA Journal,* July 1975.

[4] Kahler, Taibi. "Drivers: The Key to the Process of Scripts," *TA Journal,* July 1975.

[5] *Op.cit.* at 1.

[6] Kahler, Taibi. *Transactional Analysis Revisited,* Human Development Publications, Little Rock, 1978.

Unit Five
Phases

In 1977, I discovered Phases, which explained why some people "change," developing new motivations in life and different Distress Sequences – sequential patterns of more intense distress behavior.

Chapter 1. Base and Phase

The Phase Personality Type floor is the floor of a person's personality structure that houses his current and most important psychological need(s).[*] These psychological needs determine what motivates the person personally and professionally.

Research has validated that PTM is a unique and predictive model and the concept of the Phase Personality is the reason that this is so. When a person does not get the psychological need(s) of his Phase met positively, he will attempt to get the *same* needs met negatively, with or without awareness. This attempt is predictive and observable in the form of sequential behaviors that are comprised of three degrees of distress. These sequences of behaviors are called "Distress Sequences" and each Personality Type has a Distress Sequence that is unique.

The predictive value of PTM was one of the reasons I was hired in 1978 by Dr. Terry McGuire to assist him in the selection of astronauts at NASA. Subsequently, he used PTM

---

[*] These psychological needs are described in detail in the next Unit.

successfully for 18 more years in the selection, placement, motivation, team building, and predicting success and failure of the astronauts.

Originally, everyone's Phase Personality Type is the same as his or her Base Personality Type – located on the first floor of the personality structure. As we have seen, the Base floor always houses the strongest Channel and Perception and this remains the case throughout life. During the period in which Base and Phase are the same, Base Personality Type also determines the person's most important psychological need(s), as well as the Distress Sequence the person experiences when those needs are not met positively.

So, for example, a Base Thinker in a Thinker Phase would have the Asking Channel with Thoughts as her strongest Channel and Perception and would be motivated primarily by the Thinker psychological needs of Recognition of Work and Time Structure. The Distress Sequence would be that of a Thinker.

If a Base Thinker is in a Feeler Phase; however, then she would still have the Asking Channel with Thoughts as her strongest Channel and Perception, but she would be motivated primarily by the Feeler psychological needs of Recognition of Person and Sensory. The Distress Sequence would be that of a Feeler.

Chapter 2. Other Floor Phases

Of the over 700,000 people profiled worldwide using the PPI, 33% continue to have their Phase Personality on their Base floor, while 67% have at some point experienced a Phase change and have their Phase Personality located on another floor of their personality structure. Research also shows that Phase changes are always sequential – the change is always to the next highest floor of the condominium. As a result, those persons who have their Phase Personality on any of floors three through six of their condominium have experienced more than one Phase change. Of those profiled: 28% have their Phase on the second floor; 20% have their Phase on the third floor; 5% have their Phase on the fourth floor; 3% have their Phase on the fifth floor; and 1% have their Phase on the sixth floor.[*]

An experienced Phase, other than the Base is called a "Stage" or "Stage Personality."

Phases last from a minimum of a few years to a lifetime. No matter how many times a person Phases, the order of the his condominium remains the same, as do most other characteristics of his personality. For example, the strongest Channel, Personality Part, Perception, and character strengths are static. These all remain those of the Base Personality.

The Phase floor, wherever it is, determines: 1) the person's most important psychological need(s), and 2) the person's primary Distress Sequence.

Following a Phase change, Base psychological needs become of secondary urgency, but it remains essential to the person's well being that the Base needs be met positively. The psychological needs associated with the Personality Types on the *other* floors of the person's structure, including any Stage floors, rank in importance based on their proximity to the Base.

---

[*] "Phasing" and the reasons people Phase are covered in a later chapter.

Unit Six
Psychological Needs

In 1970 Dr. Berne in <u>Sex and Human Loving</u> identified six "hungers."[1] I clarified and researched these hungers and found statistical correlations with the six Personality Types.

Chapter 1. Berne's Hungers

One of the most common reasons for a client to come to therapy is because she is not getting the psychological needs of her Phase Personality met positively.

In 1970 Dr. Berne identified six hungers: 1) stimulus hunger, 2) recognition hunger, 3) contact hunger, 4) sexual hunger, 5) time structure hunger, and 6) incident hunger.[2] He postulated that these are the reasons for human motivation but never referred to them as psychological needs. Nor did he identify them with ego states, transactions, games, or scripts, or attempt any other behavioral correlation.

Dr. Berne used stimulus hunger to refer to the need to experience the senses. Recognition hunger was the need to be acknowledged. Contact hunger was physical touch. Sexual hunger was the drive, or need for, penetration. Time structure hunger was the need to structure time. Incident hunger was described as needing a heightened payoff.

In my 1972 doctoral dissertation research, I tested these hungers, other than the sexual hunger.[3] I knew that sexual hunger was not likely to be unique to one clustering of people. The results were too inconsistent and inconclusive to interpret with value.

It was obvious to me that recognition hunger – the need to be acknowledged – had to be separated into more definitive, mutually exclusive categories. For example, for some people being recognized for their work and achievement was very important, while for others, being recognized for just being themselves was more important. So, I created my own hypothesized hungers, called them psychological needs, and tested them in my 1972 Research.[4]

Since I was trained at Purdue University in behavioral sciences, accepting the term "stimulus hunger" to refer just to the senses didn't make sense to me. My terminology for this simply was "Sensory." I realized that this stimulus hunger for the senses and contact hunger for touching were really the same hunger but on an intensity continuum.

I kept the term "Contact" to refer to the psychological need for playful contact, either with others or the environment. This insight had come from my dissertation research and having worked with adolescents.

Time structuring was certainly important to a variety of people, so I wanted to include it in my research.

I had done TA training with Dr. Martin Groder at the Marion, Illinois, Maximum Security Prison, and I saw ample evidence of some people's need for incidence. Dr. Berne had implied a negative connotation for incidence, but I saw the change in inmates when Dr. Groder helped them get positive excitement needs met with his Asklepieion model.[5] I called this psychological need, Incidence.

I further saw that some people thrived with just the opposite of Incidence – being alone. I called this the

"Solitude" need from my experiences at the prison and my interest in Eastern meditation practices.

The results of my 1972 Research studies had shown strong, but not significant correlations between a given psychological need and one of the six data clusters that it found. I was at a loss to explain these results.

Chapter Notes

[1] Berne, Eric. *Sex in Human Loving,* Simon and Schuster, New York, 1970.

[2] *Ibid.*

[3] Kahler, Taibi. Dissertation: "Predicting Academic Underachievement in Ninth and Twelfth Grade Males with the Kahler Transactional Analysis Script Checklist," Purdue University, 1972.

[4] Kahler, Taibi. "Personality Pattern Inventory Validation Studies," Kahler Communications, Inc., 1982.

[5] Groder, Martin. "Asklepieion: An Integration of Psychotherapies," *Transactional Analysis After Eric Berne,* Harper and Row, New York, 1977.

Chapter 2. Psychological Needs and Phases

In 1977, I hypothesized that each of the six data clusters from my original research represented a single Personality Type, and that all six were present within each of us, were established in order early in life, and were motivated by a specific "psychological need" that, if not satisfied positively, would drive the individual to get it satisfied negatively. The behavioral evidence of the attempt to get this psychological need met negatively was the person's current Distress Sequence (miniscript). I resurrected my 1972 data and looked at the correlations for psychological needs and the current personality Distress Sequence (miniscript), rather than just with the cluster.

My 1982 research results identified these eight mutually exclusive and statistically significant psychological needs: Recognition of Work, Time Structure, Recognition of Conviction, Recognition of Person, Sensory, Solitude, Contact, and Incidence and correlated them to specific Phase Personalities, validating my hypothesis.[1] These are:

Personality Phase	Psychological Need
Thinker	Recognition of Work Time structure
Believer	Recognition of Conviction Recognition of Work
Feeler	Recognition of Person Sensory
Funster	Contact
Doer	Incidence
Dreamer	Solitude

Thinker Phase: Recognition of Work, Time Structure

The Thinker Phase person with the Recognition of Work need is goal oriented and achievement oriented. This person desires confirmation that what he has done is noticed. He is motivated by awards, bonuses, a pat on the back – ways of recognizing that he has done a good job.

Time Structure refers to the need for knowing what is to be done and when. People with Time Structure needs plan for today, tomorrow, and next week. When left alone to relax in the sun, a person with Time Structure need is mentally asking, "What am I going to do? What are my plans?"

Believer Phase: Recognition of Work, Recognition of Conviction

Like the Thinker Phase person, the Believer Phase person needs for her achievements to be recognized. This need is connected, however, to her strong commitment and belief in what her mission or goal is.

The Recognition of Conviction need refers to having a commitment to a belief, an opinion, or a judgment and to have this valued. It is important to people who have this need that people listen to their beliefs. They do not necessarily have to be agreed with, but they *must* be respected.

Feeler Phase: Recognition of Person, Sensory

Recognition of Person is the need for others to accept us just the way we are, without conditions or strings, or performance required. The Feeler Phase person wants other people to say that they appreciate him or like him or that they are glad that he is part of the group.

A person with the Sensory need intensely appreciates sights, smells, touches, tastes, and sounds. This person wants her environment pleasant, nice to look at, melodious, comfortable and relaxing.

Dreamer Phase: Solitude

People whose need is Solitude tend to be withdrawn, often moving into self-reflective, imaginative reveries. They are often at peace with themselves, enjoy being within themselves, and prefer alone time.

Funster Phase: Contact

People who desire an environment that "turns them on" are showing their need for Contact. Frequent interaction with others, fabrics and textures, mechanical devices, loud music, games, bright lights, and favorite posters often satisfy Contact hunger. Also, they prefer to be around fun people.

Doer Phase: Incidence

The Incidence need is a basic desire for a great deal of excitement in a short period of time. People with the Incidence need usually prefer structuring their own time for short periods of great intensity as opposed to a 9-to-5 schedule. Doer Phase people like the excitement of gambling, horse racing, high finance, selling, and the like.

The PTMP includes individualized Actions Plans for each client profiled so that the therapist can give "homework" to get these important Phase needs met positively on a daily and weekly basis, to help establish symptomatic relief and social control.[2]

Chapter Notes

[1] Kahler, Taibi. "Personality Pattern Inventory Validation Studies," Kahler Communications, Inc., 1982.
[2] Kahler, Taibi. "T.A.S.P.," Taibi Kahler Associates, Inc., 1997.

Unit Seven
The Basement: Second Degree Distress

Each of the six Personality Type Phases has a Second Degree Distress collection of negative behaviors, consisting of a behavioral life position, a mask, a failure mechanism, warning signals, a role, a myth, a cover-up feeling, games, and injunctions. All of these behaviors serve as a means of getting the Phase psychological needs met negatively.

Chapter 1. Base vs. Phase Driver: The Distress Sequence

As we saw in our discussion of Drivers, people show the Driver behavior of their Base Personality Type thousands of times a day, indicating minor distress that is the result of miscommunication. In people who have experienced a Phase Change, a substantial majority of the time that a Driver appears, it still is the Driver of the Base Personality Type. The remainder of the time, it is the Driver of the Phase Personality Type. Why?

The presentation of the Base Driver indicates miscommunication – the presentation of the Phase Driver indicates that the psychological needs of the Phase are not getting met positively. In the vast majority of cases in which the person has experienced a Phase change, the Base Driver will not devolve into a Base Distress Sequence. If the person presents her Phase Driver, however, and no intervention occurs, there is a significant risk that she will move into Second Degree Distress (and perhaps into Third Degree

117

thereafter). The Distress Sequence of the Phase Personality Type is the only Distress Sequence that normally occurs.[*]

Does this mean that we should ignore the Base Driver? No. First, in one-third of the populace, Base and Phase Personality Type remain the same and the Base Driver will be the only one presented. Second, on rare occasions, described in Unit 11, people experience the Distress Sequence of their Base. Third, and perhaps most importantly, Base First Degree Distress can lead to Phase distress in circumstances in which the person has not had his Phase psychological needs met positively. The Base distress from miscommunication can increase the possibility that the Phase Driver will appear and begin the Phase Distress Sequence. When this occurs, the transition from Base Driver to Phase Driver can happen in an instant – and the appearance of Second Degree Distress behaviors can follow just as fast.

The lesson? When you see a Driver, intervene with the Channel and Perception that correlates to the Personality Type of the Driver that you are observing.

Chapter 2. The Teeter-Totter

In the condominium, all behaviors on all floors reflect a positive/positive position of "I'm OK–You're OK." Once a person moves out of the condominium, the positives begin to

---

[*] Of course, in those who have not Phased, the distinction between Base and Phase Drivers is not helpful, as they are one and the same. However, this does not make a practical difference for the therapist – when the therapist sees a Driver, he should confront it with the Channel and Perception that are appropriate for that Driver, whether Base or Phase.

be replaced with negatives. Drivers are the beginning of, or doorway to, distress, last only a few seconds, and reflect a conditional positive position of "OK if ...." Most of the time, a person moves back into the OK behavior of the condominium after displaying a Driver. But if a person hasn't gotten his Phase psychological needs met positively to a sufficient degree, then he is likely to move into Second Degree Distress behavior – the basement of distress.

Imagine a teeter-totter or see-saw in this basement. When one person is up (OK), the other person is down (not OK). Just like this, in the basement of distress, a person's behavior reflects either "I'm OK–You're not OK" or ""I'm not OK–You're OK."

PTM is based on the belief that we are all OK and that "I'm OK–You're OK" is the only existential life position. Driver and basement life positions are behavioral, in that the behavior, not the person, can be "not OK."

This is a good time to reinforce the sequential nature of distress. It truly is a Distress Sequence. One cannot go to Second Degree Distress, the basement, without first having been, for at least a short period, in First Degree Distress, the doorway. As a result, if the therapist notices the Driver behaviors of First Degree and intervenes (using the correct Channel and Perceptual language) to invite the client out, the client likely will not go into the basement.

Chapter 3. Just Three Masks

Of all the possible distressed behaviors a person can demonstrate in Second Degree Distress, there are just three masks through which these behaviors can be exhibited: the Attacker, the Blamer, and the Drooper.[1]

Masks refer to the distressed behavior that covers up the real, OK person behind them.

Most of the time when a person "wears" one of these Second Degree masks it is because she is settling for negative Phase needs (consciously or unconsciously), when these Phase psychological needs have not been met positively. So the "gift" that a person is giving when wearing one of these masks is to advertise what they really want from us.

The difficulty in being around people who wear masks is that masks invite masks. It takes energy to side-step a mask and not move into our own basement of distress and onto the teeter-totter. Also, people in Second Degree Distress are not thinking or feeling clearly – they are not in the OK behavior of the condominium. The further into distress we go, the greater the invitation for others to put on their own masks, exhibit their own Second Degree Distress behaviors, and reinforce our masked behavior.

The Attacker mask reflects "I'm OK–You're not OK" and is like a negative critical parent. Only two Personality Type Phases in distress wear this mask: the Thinker and the Believer.[2] The verbal "parental' Attacker mask worn by the Thinker Phase person gives the message, "You're not thinking clearly," while the Believer Phase person's mask says, "You're not believing right."

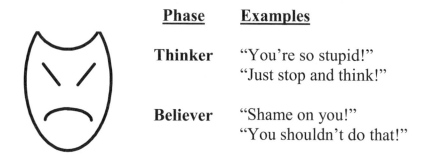

Phase	Examples
Thinker	"You're so stupid!" "Just stop and think!"
Believer	"Shame on you!" "You shouldn't do that!"

Attacker: "I'm OK–You're not OK"

The Blamer mask reflects "I'm OK–You're not OK," and is like a vengeful child. Only two Personality Type Phases in distress wear this mask: Funster and Doer.[3] The verbal vengeful mask worn by the Funster Phase person gives the message, "It's not my fault. I'm blameless." The vindictive mask worn by the Doer says, "I'm special and can bend or break the rules."

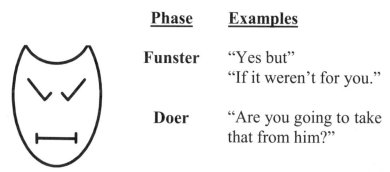

Phase	Examples
Funster	"Yes but" "If it weren't for you."
Doer	"Are you going to take that from him?"

Blamer: "I'm OK–You're not OK"

The Drooper mask reflects "I'm not OK–You're OK," and is like a victim. Only two Personality Type Phases in distress wear this mask: Feeler and Dreamer.[4] The verbal victim mask worn by the Feeler Phase person sends the message, "I'm Dumb, that was stupid," while the Dreamer Drooper-masked person just withdraws.

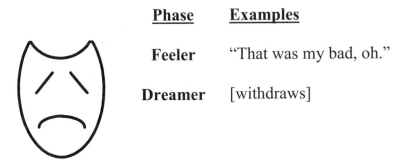

Phase	Examples
Feeler	"That was my bad, oh."
Dreamer	[withdraws]

Drooper: "I'm not OK–You're OK"

Chapter Notes

[1] Kahler, Taibi. *Process Therapy in Brief,* Human Development Publications, Little Rock, 1979.
[2] Kahler, Taibi. *Process Communication Model* [orig.], Kahler Communications, Inc., 1982.
[3] *Ibid.*
[4] *Ibid.*

Chapter 4. Failure Mechanisms

Each Personality Type Phase has a failure mechanism associated with it.[1] These mechanisms act as motifs, either to aid in getting the Phase psychological needs met negatively or to help bring into the conscious an underlying Phase issue.*

While there are only three masks that reflect Second Degree Distressed behavior within individuals, each mask is worn by two Phase Personality Types. In turn, each Phase Personality Type has a failure mechanism.

---

* Phase issues are discussed in a later chapter.

Thinker Phase persons over control; Believer Phase persons push beliefs.[2]

Funster Phase persons blame; Doer Phase persons Manipulate.[3]

Feeler Phase persons make mistakes; Dreamer Phase persons withdraw.[4]

Mask	Personality Phase	Failure Mechanism
Attacker	Thinker	Over controls
	Believer	Pushes beliefs

Thinker Phase: Over controls

Thinker Phase people know when they have done a good job and are even self starters but still have a need for Recognition of Work and Time Structure. When recognition of work, ideas, and accomplishments are not forthcoming, the distressed Thinker Phase client becomes a perfectionist, and through the Be perfect Driver over thinks for others. Then, in the basement, he over controls loved ones, colleagues and subordinates by criticizing them for not thinking clearly, mismanaging money, being irresponsible, or not being organized enough.

Just as this Thinker Phase client expects to be recognized at work for these "accurate" accountings, so does the distressed Attacker-masked Thinker expect to be thanked for being so "responsible" as "head" of the family. But family members, like others at work, hardly appreciate being micromanaged and controlled, even if the person is "correct" in the content. Masks invite masks, so the feedback verbally (or with non-verbal behavior) to the distressed Thinker is that his work is certainly recognized, but negatively.

The other psychological need for Thinker Phase people is Time Structure. They structure and plan their lives around time and expect others to adhere to exact time frames.

The client who has this Thinker Phase need will be overly sensitive to time frames. Be sure to be on time for meetings with him.

One day his spouse says, "Let's go to the movies tonight." The Thinker Phase client immediately goes into Time Structure mode to himself: "That movie has been playing for three weeks, so the lines won't be that long. There's roadwork on Main Street, so I'll need to take a five minute detour. It will take a total of twenty-two minutes to get to the theater. I'll drop honey off to get in line, while I park. I'll stand in the concession line, while honey gets the seats. I certainly don't want to sit more than five minutes before the show starts (what a waste of time), and don't want to be late. So, since the movie starts at 7:00, we have a window of departure of between 6:20 and 6:30."

If "honey" is not ready between 6:20 and 6:30, this Thinker Phase client will very likely experience negative Time Structure and might put on the Attacker mask.

Believer Phase: Pushes beliefs

Believer Phase people also know when they have done a good job and are also self starters but still have a need for Recognition of Work. When their commitment, dedication, or work is questioned or doubted, the distressed Believer Phase client becomes a perfectionist, and through the Be perfect-P Driver expects perfection of others.

One day this client's teenager proudly announces, "I got five 'A's' and a 'B'." The First Degree Distressed Believer, through her Be perfect-P Driver responds, "What exactly is the problem?" She proceeds to focus on the "B" and does not give credit for the "A's." Soon the teenager says to himself, "Will I ever be loved for myself? I can't be perfect."

The sad and ironic part of this too common occurrence is that behind the Be perfect-P mask of the Believer parent is often the commitment, "Above all I will devote my life to this child. I want him to have more than I ever dreamed of." But this commitment is sabotaged by the Driver behavior, and it is further deafened with Believer Attacker Mask lectures of: "You should be studying! You should appreciate the sacrifices we have made for you!"

The greatest praise from the Believer person is a projection of their own valued Phase needs. When positive, "I'm so proud of all the hard work you have done and all your good grades." When negative, "You should be studying! You should appreciate the sacrifices..."

For the client who projects such negative psychological needs, the painful insult to injury is that she is inviting distress in others and imposing distress on herself.

The more this client stays in her Attacker Mask, the more likely she will be considered a "poor example of a parent" by most: negative Recognition of Work. And her teenager, unless well-adjusted otherwise, may "teeter-totter" in the basement with his parent's Attacker Mask and end up with "poor grades in life."

The more important psychological need of the Believer Phase person is Recognition of Conviction. When Believers express their opinions, they are interested in others listening, hopefully even agreeing with them.

When Believer Phase people express their convictions, they are expressing a value system that is most likely underlying a mission in life. Therefore, these people often become active in community service, volunteer politics, mentoring, foster parenting, or religious activities.

Whereas opinions may be positive, being opinionated is considered negative. While having strong convictions is positive when accepting others as OK, being prejudiced indicates "pre-judging" and that the person is "not OK." Believers wear an Attacker Mask with the conviction that those who do not believe the same as they do are "not OK."

These clients push their beliefs, preach at others, scold, or negatively crusade. If they perceive that we have not heard them, they often escalate their Attacker Masks. If they do not get their Phase Recognition of Conviction needs met positively, they will get them met negatively, pushing their beliefs down someone's throat.

As with the escalations of any Personality Phase, those of the Believer can be devastating when taken to extremes. The greater the time in Second Degree Distress, the more the contaminated thinking. Potentially, in the Believer Phase basement, the following will occur: "If you do not believe the way I believe, you are not with me. If you are not with me, you are against me. If you are against me, then I will get rid of you before (I believe) you get rid of me." In business, this may be relegated to power play dismissals only. In the world, this may end life with terrorism, pogroms, crusades, jihads...

126

"It is *so* important that you believe the way I do, that if you don't, I will kill you."

Mask	Personality Phase	Failure Mechanism
Blamer	Funster	Blames
	Doer	Manipulates

Funster Phase: Blames

Funster Phase people need playful Contact from others and their environment. To understand why the failure mechanism of a distressed Funster is blaming, and how it fits in Funsters settling for negative Contact needs, a discussion of Myths is valuable. All Myths relate to the belief that each person is not solely in control of whether or not he or she feels good or bad emotionally.[*]

The Funster's Driver is Try hard. Translated into a Myth, this "not understanding" behavior becomes: "You are supposed to do the thinking for me and make me feel good."

In the Second Degree basement, the Funster unconsciously believes the Myths and wears the Blamer Mask, "It's your fault that I feel bad because you didn't make me feel good. So, I'll make you feel worse. As long as I blame you, I don't have to take responsibility for my own thoughts, actions, and feelings."

The opposite of getting playful Contact is getting negative Contact. The payoff for a distressed Funster is to believe he "made" a Thinker or Believer feel frustrated.

---

[*] See Chapter 7 in this unit for a complete description of the four Myths.

If I have not played enough with my Funster child, and frequently lectured her through my Thinker Attacker Mask about the importance of education, then it should be no surprise that I get calls from her school principal about her disruptive behavior (negative Contact).

If I have not provided my Funster with much Contact, and frequently preached at him through my Believer Attacker Mask about family values, and the belief that our family affairs should be trusted to privacy, then I should not be surprised to be saying the following on the phone: "Hello. You're Sergeant Wert? My son's been arrested? Bring clothes? He was streaking across the Governor's lawn.... CNN was there.... He was yelling, 'I am the son of _____!'" That's negative Contact. Funsters are experts at reflecting our basement Masks back at us.

A family consisting of a Believer–Thinker (Base–Phase) father and a Feeler–Believer (Base–Phase) mother bring their teenage Funster–Funster (Base–Phase) son for family therapy. He is the "identified patient" because he "always breaks the rules."

"Just this morning we found his shoes left in the living room. He knows the rules. We signed a written contract regarding all of our behavior. Right here on page nineteen, paragraph three, we all agree 'to pick up our things and put them away in our rooms if we are leaving a room for more than sixty minutes.' Doctor, how much more fair can it be? We are only asking him to do what we are also agreeing to do."

The first thing parents need to understand about their child is what Personality Type Base and Phase she is. Knowing the Base Type provides the magic wand of communication: the Perceptual language to speak and the Channel to use. Knowing the Phase provides the insight to negative behavior and the key to motivation.

Parents also need to understand the difference between symptoms and the problem. Leaving the shoes in the living room is only one of hundreds of possible symptoms of the distressed Funster. What's important to the parents? If it's cleaning up, he's messy. If it's locking the doors, he leaves them open. If it's turning off the lights, he leaves them on. If it's feeding the dog, he forgets. If it's looking "respectable," he gets a mohawk and piercings. If.., then…. The key here is negative Contact.

THE SHOES ARE NOT THE PROBLEM. *Whenever we are in 2nd degree basement behavior, it has nothing to do with the apparent content.*

The shoes are but a symptom of the real problem that the son is not getting enough playful Contact needs met positively.

Let's look at why these parents were not successful with expecting their "fair" contract to work. Thinker and Believer parents seem predisposed to offer contracts. Why? Because it is a logical and fair (Thinker), and just and right (Believer), way of dealing with a problem. And, it meets the psychological needs of Recognition of Work for these Thinker and Believer Phase parents. But does it meet the needs of their Funster teenager? No. How can we expect someone to stop a behavior without replacing it with something positive? And remember, the distressed Funster gets a negative Contact payoff seeing Thinkers and Believers become frustrated.

Far too many Funsters in distress are assessed as having ADHD than merit the diagnosis, as most all of the classical symptoms match a healthy, normal Funster whose playful psychological needs simply are not getting met positively.[5]

The key to dealing with this distressed Funster Phase teenager is his psychological need for playful Contact. We all have a natural tendency to assume that what works for us should work for others. Let's look at each Personality Type parent.

We have already seen that Thinker and Believer parents prefer a contract because it involves thinking, commitment, and a measurable plan of achievement – but neither is the problem addressed nor is positive Contact given as a replacement. The result – shoes left in the room and parents who are frustrated.

Feeler parents are prone to Rescuing – over taking care of. "Oh, there are his shoes. He must have forgotten to put them away. He's so tired, I won't wake him up. I'll just put his shoes away for him." No positive Contact replacement here either. The result – shoes and socks left in the room the next night. Such continued Rescuing will reinforce the following message, when (if) this teenager grows up: "Just wait for someone to do your job for you." This loving Feeler parent has good intentions but slipped into over-caring.

The Doer parent is direct: "Take your shoes to your room." Funster: "I don't know why I have to…. Mom took Mary's shoes to her room for her…" After receiving the Directing Channel with Actions Perception from the Doer every night, and continued complaining from the distressed Funster, the Doer explodes with negative excitement: "I told you to take those #!*!# shoes to your room!" No positive Contact here. The result: shoes are put in the room only when the Funster is confronted and threatened. Since the ultimate threat from the Doer can be physical, the Funster may conclude, "The strongest gets what he wants in life."

The Dreamer parent may point out that the shoes have not been put away, but since this Type does not offer the "frustration" payoff to the Funster, the shoes may or may not be put away.

There are two aspects of dealing with the Funster–Funster: intervention and prevention. Intervention means giving bite-size offerings of playful Contact, instead of negative needs or even the wrong positive psychological needs.

With the shoes, an example of a bite-size offering of playful Contact could be putting a note in the shoe: "I'm so lonely for my friends in the closet." This "confronts" the negative behavior, but in a playful way that the Funster can hear. Also, there is wisdom in knowing what not to do. In the above examples of the different Personality Type parents, their preferred solutions certainly didn't work because the parents focused on the symptoms (warning signals) and not on the problem (psychological need).

Prevention charges the Phase batteries, so that the Funster doesn't have to do things to get negative Contact. A simple formula is to spend at least twenty minutes a day with the Funster Phase teenager doing what she or he wants to do for playful Contact (fun). The same sex parent connection seems to be of particular value.

Behavioral consequences can also be valuable, as long as the confrontations are in the Playful Channel with Reactions (likes/dislikes) as the Perception. One could, for example, establish that the Funster may have his room decorated the way he wants and can afford, but he may neither leave food overnight in the room nor have it smell so bad as to be noticeable immediately upon entering. The consequence of either is loss of phone privileges for a week.

Be prepared to "confront" old symptoms, especially before the positive batteries are all charged up. Funsters tend to test boundaries. When these transgressions occur, do not sabotage with the Thinker or Believer Asking Channel and Thoughts/Opinions Perceptions: "Do you remember our agreement. I believe we said...." Do not sabotage with the Feeler Comforting Channel and Emotions Perception: "Oh, honey. I feel so bad about this...." Do not sabotage with the Doer Directing Channel and Actions Perception: "Go get your phone and give it to me."

Instead, use the Funster Playful Channel with Reactions (likes/dislikes) Perception: "Hope you like the Seven Eleven and got lots of quarters. No phono for a weeko." This "confronts" and gives the message of the behavioral consequence. And no payoff of "You got me frustrated."

Doer Phase: Manipulates

Thinker and Believer Phase individuals can postpone gratification. Funster and Doer Phase individuals need immediate gratification. In particular, Doer Phase people need positive Incidence – a great deal of excitement in a short period of time. Negative Incidence results from manipulating others or the situation, for a rush or immediate gratification.

132

A Believer–Doer chemist so believes that he has discovered a cure for cancer that he takes a second mortgage on his home, takes the family savings, and loses it all on one role of the dice in Vegas in order to finance his research.

A Doer–Doer politician gets caught in a brothel by the same paparazzi whom he challenged to catch him doing something wrong.

A Feeler–Doer movie star returning from receiving an Academy Award is arrested for driving 120 mph in a hospital zone and for possession of a gram of cocaine in her Ferrari.

A Funster–Doer All Pro football player is caught betting on his own games.

A Thinker–Doer personal financial advisor uses clients' monies in her own day trading account.

A Believer–Doer manager constantly pits his employees against one another, resulting in negative competition, a climate of hostility, and an environment of crisis after crisis.

Mask	Personality Phase	Failure Mechanism
Drooper	Feeler	Makes Mistakes
	Dreamer	Withdraws

Feeler Phase: Makes Mistakes

All of these failure mechanisms are consistently recurring behaviors that are unique to a Personality Type Phase when in Second Degree Distress. In other words, we all make mistakes, but it is the Feeler Phase person whose failure mechanism will repeatedly be "Make mistakes" in Second Degree Distress, no matter how intelligent the person is.

Why? Because each person is driven to get Phase psychological needs met negatively when they are not met positively.

Feeler Phase people are motivated by the psychological needs of Recognition of Person and Sensory. When this person does not arrange or get enough of these needs met positively, then with or without awareness she will be driven to get these same needs met negatively.

A typical example of this Distress Sequence is the following. The Feeler Phase client has over adapted to a loved one. She has agreed to do something that she cannot or does not want to do but agreed to it through her Please you Driver. Unconsciously, she then makes a mistake, and when this is brought to her attention, she takes it personally (internalizes), and experiences "You're criticizing me – there's something wrong with me." Negative Recognition of Person. She wanted to be unconditionally accepted as a person (Phase need), but she unconsciously arranged to get (interpret) just the opposite. Feelers wearing a Drooper mask have difficulty separating their behavior from themselves and take things too personally. That's why pointing out negative behavior, however accurate or how "OK" it is delivered, is experienced by the distressed Feeler Phase person as a personal attack.

Feeler Phase people also need their senses attended to. Most of us have use of all of our five senses – sight, taste, touch, hearing, and smell. For Feeler Phase individuals, these senses are more than physiological phenomena; they are psychological motivators.

So, distressed Feeler Phase clients set themselves up to get this need met negatively. They don't get touched enough, or worse, get hurt. They don't wear their favorite colognes or perfumes. They let their appearance slip. They overeat. They let their environment get dirty or disheveled. They "let themselves go."

Dreamer Phase: Withdraws

Dreamer Phase people have a need for solitude. Recall that the most important needs to get met are those of the Phase. Phase needs provide energy to move the elevator to the various floors of the condominium.

A Persister–Feeler husband and Thinker–Dreamer wife come to see you for marriage counseling. Their presenting problems are that "He smothers me with all his feelings," and "She keeps rejecting me."

In your session with him, you discover that he has recently Phased to Feeler, and he is now motivated by wanting to share his feelings, have a deeper emotional connection with his wife, and be around her more often. When rebuffed, he now feels rejected and sometimes unloved.

In your session with her, she explains that he is "a different person" ever since the death of his mother, who had lived with them for several years while dying from cancer. "He felt so responsible for her care." Although a physician, his specialty was not oncology.

She reports that now he constantly wants to be with her and talk about his feelings. She used to be able to have her own space and alone time, but he keeps seeking her out. She feels smothered by all his attention, so she pulls away just to get a break from him.

Your assessment of them is that they have no clinical diagnosis. Since they both have a strong Computer, you give them their Action Plans from their PTMP report on how each one can get his Phase needs met on a daily and weekly basis. You explain the importance of this and the consequences.

With them both in the room, you say to him (Believer Base): "Do you believe she loves you?" He responds, "Yes." "Now that you have read about her Dreamer Phase needs, do you believe she has her own needs for alone time and privacy?" He responds, "Yes."

To her (Thinker Base), "Do you understand that he is in a Feeler Phase and needs more intimacy and closeness because he loves you so much?" She responds, "Yes."

"You both love one another and want to make your marriage stronger. Here's your homework: Will you each get your Phase needs met without relying on the other person this week and together come up with a plan to help each other get Phase needs met? Responses: "Yes."

The following week they present you with their plan. She explains, "He is going to have a gazebo built for me. When I want to get my solitude needs met, I'll go there by myself. That will energize me to use my elevator to go to my Feeler floor more often when he wants to share feelings and be close. That will help his Feeler Phase."

You say to him, "Do you believe that will help her get her Dreamer Phase needs met?" He responds, "Yes." "Do you also believe that she will then be more open to your feelings?" He responds, "Yes, I believe she will be."

"Before, you felt as if she were rejecting you when she would go away by herself. What do you believe you will feel when she goes to her gazebo and doesn't want you to join her?"

"She should do what she needs to do. And in my opinion she is not rejecting me. I now believe just the opposite. She's going into herself, not away from me. The more she feels better about herself, the more she will want to be with me. I believe it's a good thing. I won't feel rejected, I'll feel hopeful."

"So, you both will be getting your needs met."

Sometimes just "information" therapy is valuable, especially when working with a Believer and Thinker Base couple.

Chapter Notes

[1] Kahler, Taibi. *Process Communication Model,* Kahler Communications, Inc., Little Rock, 1982.
[2] *Ibid.*
[3] *Ibid.*
[4] *Ibid.*
[5] Bailey, Rebecca. Dissertation. "An investigation of Personality Types of adolescents who have been rated by classroom teachers to exhibit Inattentive and/or Hyperactivity-Impulse Behaviors," University of Arkansas, 1998.

Chapter 5. Warning Signals

The following table shows the warning signals for each Personality Phase:

Phase Type	Warning Signals
Thinker:	Frustrated with those who don't think
	Critical around time, money, and responsibility
Believer:	Frustrated with those who do not believe the same
	Critical or suspicious
Funster:	Negative and complaining
	Easily bored or vengeful
Doer:	Sets up arguments
	Creates negative drama
	Ignores or breaks the rules
Feeler:	Invites criticism
	Denigrates self
	Shows self doubt
Dreamer:	Passively waits
	Projects started but not finished
	Feels inadequate or embarrassed

These warning signals indicate that the person is not getting his or her Phase psychological needs met positively.

Chapter 6. Roles

As I said in the introduction, I consider Dr. Steve Karpman's Drama Triangle[1] to be a profound contribution to understanding interactional dynamics in distressed situations.

Steve identified three Roles that define the Drama Triangle: Victim, Persecutor, and Rescuer. The "drama" of life when distress is involved can be explained by how we take on these roles with others – by being a Victim and acting helpless, by being a Persecutor and attacking others, or by being a Rescuer and overdoing for others.

Four "attractions" to symbioses can be identified: a Victim in search of a Rescuer [V→R]; a Rescuer in search of a Victim [R→V]; a Victim in search of a Persecutor [V→P]; and a Persecutor in search of a Victim [P→V].

Four of the Personality Phases in the basement reflect the Role of Persecutor in search of a Victim: Thinker, Believer, Funster, and Doer. One Personality Phase there reflects the Role of Victim in search of a Persecutor: the Feeler. The Dreamer is in the Victim role, but does not advertise for rescue or persecution.

Chapter Notes

[1] Karpman, Stephen. "Fairy Tales and Script Drama analysis," *Transactional Analysis Bulletin,* April 1968.

Chapter 7. Myths

I consider the four Myths (Four Fallacies) to be among the most important, if not most basic discoveries that I have made.[1]

Dr. Berne cautioned that a theory/model was not complete until it could be explained in eight-year old language. Certainly Steve Karpman's Drama Triangle reflects such genius and simplicity.

I conceived of the idea of the Four Myths in 1972 and wanted to be able to say in simple language how we further negative behavior transactionally:

<u>Four Myths</u>

"I believe I can make you feel good emotionally." [R→V]

"I believe you can make me feel good emotionally." [V→R]

"I believe I can make you feel bad emotionally." [P→V]

"I believe you can make me feel bad emotionally." [V→P]

These Myths are at the base for justifying staying in maladaptive behavior.

The "make feel good" Myths have a foundation in the Drivers at First Degree. The "make feel bad" Myths are found in the basement of Second Degree.

A caution to fellow therapists: casual expressions may be interpreted consciously or unconsciously by the client as permissions to continue to believe in one or more of the Myths.

Examples of such expressions by therapists include:

"How did that make you feel?"

"Did that make you angry?"

"And that hurt your feelings."

"Did that bother you?"

"Did that embarrass you?"

"I'll bet that made you feel so good."

We can invite others to feel good or bad, but we can't make them feel good or bad emotionally. "No one can make you feel inferior without your consent." Eleanor Roosevelt.

Chapter Notes

[1] Kahler, Taibi. *Transactional Analysis Revisited,* Human Development Publications, Little Rock, 1978.

Chapter 8. Cover-up Feelings

Through the years, different theorists have postulated a list of "authentic, healthy, OK" feelings, as well as lists of cover-up feelings (called rackets in TA)[1] that would describe everyone.

"Mad" and "sad" seemed to make everybody's lists, but indiscriminately on either the healthy or the cover-up. One of the reasons for this confusion is that these can be either, depending upon whether the emotion is experienced in the condominium or in distress.

"Mad," for example, is a life freeing, healthy emotion, especially for Feelers, when experienced in the condominium, but a pushing-others-away, cover-up feeling for Thinkers in their basement. So, we cannot list "mad" as either a healthy or cover-up emotion, without putting it in personality dynamic context.

The following cover-up feelings, correlated to each Personality Phase are experienced in the basement of Second Degree:[2]

Personality Phase	Cover-up Feeling
Thinker	Frustratedly angry
Believer	Righteously angry
Funster	Vengeful
Doer	Vindictive
Feeler	Sad
Dreamer	Insignificant

I distinguish vengeful from vindictive by reference to intent and intensity. The Funster's vengefulness is a reactive, instinctive slap, "giving as good as I got." The Doer's vindictiveness is a calculated revenge, "so that you will never cross me again."

Chapter Notes

[1] Berne, Eric. *Principles of Group Treatment,* Oxford University Press, New York, 1966.
[2] Kahler, Taibi. "Personality Pattern Inventory Validity Studies," Kahler Communications, Inc., 1982.

Chapter 9. Games

In 1961, Dr. Berne defined games as having an orderly series of transactions, an ulterior aspect, and a payoff.[1] By 1970, Berne had developed "Formula G:"

$$C+G=R \rightarrow S \rightarrow X \rightarrow P$$

(Con+Gimmick=Response→Switch→Crossup→Payoff).[2]

The Switch was added by Dr. Berne to emphasize the role changes in the Karpman Drama Triangle.[3] In the Drama Triangle, Drivers at First Degree Distress take on the role of Rescuer looking for a Victim, or Victim advertising for a Rescuer. A switch in roles occurs when moving into Second Degree Distress. Droopers (only Feelers, not Dreamers) take on the role of a Victim advertising for a Persecutor, while Attackers and Blamers take on the role of Persecutor looking for a Victim. Notice the two types of victims, depending on the degree of distress.

In both the 1974 miniscript article and *Transactional Analysis Revisited,* I diagrammed these moves in games using the miniscript, showing that all games start with a Driver at the Con and Gimmick level, and progress to Second Degree at the Response, Switch, Crossup, and Payoff.[4,5]

The implications for this integration of games into miniscript and now PTM is that clinicians do not need to memorize the dozens and dozens of games to recognize and stop the beginning moves of a game. Rather they need to know only how to identify the six Driver behaviors and know the appropriate intervention (confrontational) strategies for them.[*]

When appropriate, you might want to teach your client how to side-step Games at the Gimmick level by focusing on Drivers, Channels, and Perceptions.

Games cannot be ascribed just to a given Personality Type or "Adaptation." Which games people play depends on additional factors as well; for example, whether the person

---

[*] *See* Unit 3, Chapter 10.

has Phased, how many times, and what the order of her condominium is.

I agree with Dr. Berne's Formula G, and I believe that most "games" labeled as such in TA literature are not actually Games, as they do not conform to this formula.

Chapter Notes

[1] Berne, Eric. *Transactional Analysis in Psychotherapy,* Grove Press, New York, 1961.
[2] Berne, Eric. *What Do You say After You Say Hello,* Grove Press, New York, 1972.
[3] Karpman, Stephen. "Fairy Tales and Script Drama Analysis," *Transactional Analysis Bulletin,* April 1968.
[4] Kahler, Taibi with Hedges Capers. "The Miniscript," *TA Journal,* January 1974.
[5] Kahler, Taibi. *Transactional Analysis Revisited,* Human Development Publications, Little Rock, 1978.

Chapter 10. Injunctions

In 1966 Dr. Claude Steiner coined the TA term "injunction," referring to a negative message that prohibits or inhibits the free behavior of the individual.[1] He also theorized how parents passed these on to their children. His work is inspiring, and, in PTM, it is explained as parents *reinforcing* innate Personality Type injunctions, rather than "passing them on."

Dr. Bob and Mary Goulding originally identified ten of these primary injunctions: "don't be," "don't be you," "don't be a child," "don't grow," "don't make it," "don't be important," "don't belong," "don't be well (sane)," "don't think," and "don't feel."[2] Three were subsequently added by them: "don't be close (sexual)," "don't succeed," and "don't want" (and the lethal version, "don't need"). The Gouldings also associated the probable resulting behaviors of each of these, as well as discovering one of the most useful models of psychotherapy with which to deal with them: Redecision Therapy.

In *Transactional Analysis Revisited,* I showed the integration sequentially of the miniscript both structurally and functionally, identifying First Degree Drivers as the functional manifestations of structural counterscripts and Second Degree Stoppers as the functional manifestations of these structural injunctions.[3]

The results of the 1972 and 1982 research studies supported the importance of the injunctions: these injunctions correlate to Base Personality Type but change as a function of a different Phase. The exact way in which they change depends on the structure of the client's personality condominium.[4]

This is particularly important because a therapist should not assume a simple correlation exists between a given Personality Type (or Adaptation) and one or more injunctions. That assumption is ***only valid*** if the individual has not Phased.

The purpose of the injunction is to reinforce the issue of the Phase.[*] For example, "Don't grow up" is the primary injunction for the Funster. This injunction serves to inhibit further a Phasing Funster from dealing with his Phase issue of taking responsibility for his emotions and actions.

Each Personality Type has a primary injunction associated with it. But because personality structure is

---

[*] Phase issues are discussed in detail in Unit 9.

145

composed of a stacking of Personality Types and the Phase floor changes one or more times in two-thirds of the population, one should not assume that a given Personality Type (or Adaptation/diagnostic label) therefore has this correlated injunction. The product of Phasing sometimes "deactivates" the injunction. The following diagram gives the correlations of the Base Personality Type and the primary and secondary injunctions.

Personality Types and Injunction Correlations

Base Type	Primary	Secondary
Dreamer	Don't make it	Don't belong Don't have fun Don't be close Don't be important
Doer	Don't be close	Don't trust Don't make it Don't belong
Believer	Don't trust	Don't be close Don't enjoy Don't belong
Feeler	Don't feel anger	Don't be important Don't grow up
Funster	Don't grow up	Don't make it Don't be close
Thinker	Don't feel grief	Don't have fun Don't be close Don't enjoy

Consider a Thinker in a Funster Phase. Although a Base Funster would have a primary injunction of "Don't grow up," a Base Thinker in a Funster Phase (Thinker–Funster) would not have this injunction. Why not? Because the Thinker "has grown up" (in fact, always was grown up), because her Thoughts Perception permeates her world through her Computer, aided by character traits of being responsible, logical, and organized.

As the PTMP would report on this client, this Thinker–Funster would have no primary injunction, but interestingly, she would have a carry-over secondary Base injunction of "Don't enjoy." This would alert the therapist as to why this client is not likely to be totally successful in getting her Funster psychological need of Contact met positively. She can have fun, but not continue the enjoyment. And, if she is not dealing with the Phase issue of responsibility, she is using the lack of joy as fuel to blame someone else.

Chapter Notes

[1] Steiner, Claude. "Scripts and Counterscripts," *Transactional Analysis Bulletin*, 1966.
[2] Goulding, Robert and Mary. "Injunctions, Decisions, and Redecisions," *TA Journal,* 1976.
[3] Kahler, Taibi. *Transactional Analysis Revisited,* Human Development Publication, Little Rock, 1978.
[4] Kahler, Taibi. "Personality Pattern Inventory Validation Studies," Kahler Communications, Inc., 1982.

Chapter 11. Scripts

A process Script is a false belief originating in Drivers, reinforced through sentence patterns, and replayed throughout life in intensity as a function of distress.[1]

As was discussed in Unit Four, Scripts are formed at First Degree Distress by Drivers through sentence (thought) patterns and are reinforced in intensity in Second Degree Distress. So the more time a person stays in the Second

Degree basement of distress, the more his Script becomes a problem. And since a person experiences this basement distress most often in Phase, the Script of the Phase is the most important. As long as a person does not go into the basement or cellar of Base Distress, the Base Script will cause him no further problem in his life. It will merely be reinforced at First Degree through sentence structure.

Scripts on the Assessing Matrix

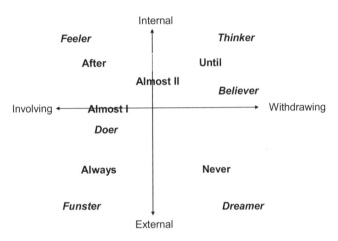

Scripts are valuable to the Process Therapist, as they are accurate predictors of how a client may sabotage not only his therapy, but also his life.

The previous diagram shows the Scripts that correlate directly with Personality Type (and in two instances Base/Phase combinations) on the Assessing Matrix with the Personality Types.[2]

After Script

Feelers have an After Script. They are afraid that something bad will happen. Interestingly this becomes a self-fulfilling prophecy because the person likely has over adapted (Please you) and, in so doing, set herself up to be a victim.

Until Script

Thinkers and Believers have an Until Script. They postpone gratification, with an attitude of "I can't have fun until." They constantly put work or accomplishments first, driven by perfection.

Always Script

Funsters and Doers have an Always Script and feel trapped or cornered in life. Funsters stay cornered, blaming and waiting for someone to rescue them. Doers feel cornered and manipulate others into the corner.

Never Script

Dreamers have a Never Script. They have difficulty having closure with projects in life, especially when an important independent decision is required.

Almost I Script

Funsters in Feeler Phase and Feelers in Funster Phase have an Almost I Script. They almost complete a task, but not quite.

Almost II Script

Thinkers and Believers in Feeler Phase, and Feelers in either Thinker Phase or Believer Phase, have an Almost II Script. They do complete tasks or goals, but then they have the problems. This Script manifests differently depending on whether it is in a professional or personal context.

Professional: A "professional" Almost II Script is experienced as completing the goal or task, but if it was done with the person experiencing considerable distress (*e.g.*, in the basement), then the "achievement" won't last. The reason for the inevitable failure can be attributed to the Phase Distress Sequence. For example, if this Almost II (professional) Script person's Phase was Thinker, then the degeneration of the project will have resulted from morale problems with his colleagues and/or subordinates who weren't given important tasks (Be perfect: not delegating) and were threatened and micromanaged (Attacker Mask: over controlling).

Personal: People with an Almost II (personal) Script have achieved "all they want" in their personal life: a spouse, two kids, a house with a white picket fence, family pet.... But their experience is, "Is this all there is?"

Chapter Notes

[1] Kahler, Taibi. "T.A.S.P. Guide for Therapists," Taibi Kahler Associates, Inc., 1997.
[2] Kahler, Taibi. *Process Communication Model* [orig.], Kahler Communication, Inc., 1982.

Chapter 12. Meeting Phase Needs Negatively.

Each of the Second Degree Distress behaviors is an unconscious means of getting psychological needs of the Personality Phase met negatively.

Masks reinforce the behavioral life positions through their associated behaviors.

Failure mechanisms are motifs furthered by warning signals.

Myths are justifications delivered through Roles and cover-up feelings.

Injunctions are inhibitions to positive Phase needs.

Games are First and Second Degree interactions that can involve masks, behavioral life positions, failure mechanisms, warning signals, Myths, roles, cover-up feelings, and injunctions.

Scripts are recurring failure patterns connecting First and Second Degree distress.

The following descriptions of the Phase types show how Second Degree Distress generates negative psychological needs of the same Phase.[1]

The Thinker Phase
Psychological Needs Are
Recognition of Work and Time Structure

Negative Recognition of Work and Time Structure are generated by the basement behaviors and reinforced by the theme: "You're not thinking clearly, so you can't get your work done, and you're wasting time."

Mask/life position

Attacker - "I'm OK–You're not OK"

Failure mechanism/warning signals

Over controls
Frustrated with those who don't "think"
Critical around time, money, and responsibility

Myths, Roles, Cover-up Feelings

"I can make you feel bad emotionally." Persecutor. Frustratedly angry.

Injunctions

"Don't feel grief." "Don't have fun."[*]

Script

Until: "Can't have fun until the work is done."

Movie: Peter Banning in *Hook*. Thinker Phase negative Recognition of Work when he gets the phone call from Brad, and his son "shoots" him. He yells "Shut up!"

Movie: Chuck Noland in *Cast Away*. Thinker Phase negative Time Structure at beginning of movie. He lectures at them about lost time.

The Believer Phase
Psychological Needs are Recognition of Work and Recognition of Conviction

Negative Recognition of Work and Recognition of Conviction are generated by the basement behaviors and reinforced by the theme: "You're not listening to my opinions or believing the right way, so you won't get your mission accomplished."

---

[*] For all Personality Phases, the injunctions and Scripts listed apply only for persons who have not experienced a Phase change. In each case, the change will alter these characteristics. The PTMP report automatically generates the appropriate Script and Injunctions for any of the 4,320 Base, Phase and ordering combinations.

Mask/life position

Attacker - "I'm OK–You're not OK"

Failure mechanism/warning signals

Pushes beliefs.
Frustrated with those who don't believe the same.
Critical and suspicious.

Myths, Roles, Cover-up Feelings

"I can make you feel bad emotionally." Persecutor.
Righteously angry.

Injunctions

"Don't trust." "Don't enjoy."

Script

Until: "Can't enjoy until the mission is done"

Movie: Colonel Jessup in *A Few Good Men.* Believer Phase negative Recognition of Conviction with lecture: "You can't handle the truth!"

Movie: Lieutenant Dan in *Forrest Gump.* Believer Phase negative Recognition of Work with his lecture in the hospital: "I had a destiny. I was Lieutenant Dan Taylor."

The Funster Phase
Psychological Need is Contact

Negative Contact is generated by the basement behaviors and reinforced by the theme: "I'll show you!"

Mask/life position

Blamer - "I'm OK–You're not OK"

Failure mechanism/warning signals

Blames.
Negative and complaining.
Easily bored.

Myths, Roles, Cover-up Feelings

"You made me feel bad emotionally, so I'll make you feel worse." Persecutor. Vengeful.

Injunctions

"Don't grow up." "Don't make it."

Script

Always: "Someone [life] cornered me, so I'll wait there to 'make them feel worse.'"

Movie: Short Round in *Indiana Jones and the Temple of Doom*. Funster Phase negative Contact when Indiana tells him, "Don't touch anything." He does and says, "It's not my fault."

The Doer Phase
Psychological Need is Incidence

Negative Incidence is generated by the basement behaviors and reinforced by the theme: "I'm special."

Mask/life position

Blamer - "I'm OK–You're not OK"

Failure mechanism/warning signals

Manipulates.
Sets up arguments.
Creates negative drama.

Ignores or breaks the rules.

Myths, Roles, Cover-up Feelings

"You made me feel bad emotionally, so I'll make you feel horrible." Persecutor. Vindictive.

Injunctions

"Don't be close." "Don't belong."

Script

Always: "Someone cornered me, so I'll corner them."

Movie: Buddy Love in *The Nutty Professor* (1996). Doer Phase negative Incidence when Buddy is on his date at the comedy club and "Makes a fool of" the attacking comic.

The Feeler Phase
Psychological Needs Are
Recognition of Person and Sensory

Negative Recognition of Person and Sensory are generated by the basement behaviors and reinforced by the theme: "There's something wrong with me. I don't even deserve sensual pleasures."

Mask/life position

Drooper - "I'm not OK–You're OK"

Failure mechanism/warning signals

Makes mistakes.
Invites criticism.
Denigrates self.
Shows self doubt.

Myths, Roles, Cover-up Feelings

"You made me feel bad emotionally." Victim. Sad.

Injunctions

"Don't feel angry." "Don't grow up."

Script

After: "Things are going too well-something bad is going to happen to me."

Movie: Prof. Klump in *The Nutty Professor* (1996). Feeler Phase negative Recognition of Person when he is on his date at the comedy club and plays "Kick Me" and Sensory when he is home over-eating.

The Dreamer Phase
Psychological Need Is Solitude

Negative solitude is generated by the basement behaviors and reinforced by the theme: "I'm shutting down, even from external directions."

Mask/life position

Drooper - "I'm not OK–You're OK"

Failure mechanism/warning signals

Passively waits.
Projects started but not finished.
Feels inadequate or embarrassed.

Myths, Roles, Cover-up Feelings

"Things or people can make me feel bad emotionally." Victim. Unimportant.

<u>**Injunctions**</u>

"Don't make it." "Don't be important."

<u>**Script**</u>

Never: "I never get anything finished."

Movie: Forrest Gump in *Forrest Gump*. Dreamer Phase negative Solitude after Jenny visits – he withdraws inward.

Chapter Notes

1. Kahler, Taibi. *Process Communication Model* [orig.], Kahler Communications, Inc., 1982.

Chapter 13. Intervening at Second Degree.

As we have seen, the way to stay out of Second Degree Distress is to make sure that the psychological needs of our Phase are met positively on a regular basis. It is far more effective if this is the case in both our personal and our professional lives.

All we have to do is look around us to see that this does not happen all, or even most, of the time for many people. We see people in Second Degree Distress every day. The good news is that while going into distress is always sequential – you can't be in Second Degree without first being in First Degree and you can't be in Third Degree without first being in Second Degree – we can come out at any time without traveling through the prior levels. How do we go about intervening to invite people out of the basement? We give them an invitation out by helping them to get their psychological needs met positively.

For example, when confronted with the attacking Thinker, we find a way to provide her with positive Recognition of Work.

Thinker: "Doesn't anyone around here know how to think clearly? We have to finish the project on time and it has to be done right!"

Answer: "We certainly appreciate how hard you've worked on this and we definitely will do our part. Thank you for your leadership."

Thinker: "You're welcome."

By showing the attacking Thinker that you recognize her competence, you invite her out of distress.

What about the other Personality Types? The same techniques apply. Provide the Doer with positive Incidence by providing him a short term reward. The Feeler can be provided positive Recognition of Person by being told how glad we are to have him on the team. The Funster can be provided Contact by being given an opportunity to listen to her mp3 player or take a break from work. The Believer can have his Recognition of Conviction needs met positively by being told that his opinion is respected even if it is not agreed with. The Dreamer can be provided with "away time" to sit and reflect and get her Solitude need met.

These are but a few of many ways in which we can act to help our distressed clients, friends and colleagues. In both PTM and PCM training seminars, participants are given the opportunity to explore other ways to achieve this end. A few further examples are found in Appendix F.

Unit Eight
The Cellar: Third Degree Distress

Third Degree Distress is the final "payoff" of the negative psychological needs, experienced by the Despairer mask in a give-up position. Occupying the cellar requires first having been in the basement, and before that the doorway – the Driver.

Chapter 1. Dynamics

The cellar houses the Despairer mask and reflects, "I'm not OK–You're not OK."[1]

The longer a client spends in the cellar, the more difficult it is to think clearly, to feel authentically, and to function effectively.

The basement represents attempts to get the Phase psychological needs met negatively. When even that doesn't work, the person slips into a give-up position and feels depressed.

Chapter Notes

[1] Kahler, Taibi. *Process   Therapy in Brief*, Human Development Publications, Little Rock, 1979.

Chapter 2. Depression

Because of the lingering effects of not meeting the Phase psychological needs, even negatively, in the basement of Second Degree Distress, the resulting cellar depressions are experienced differently.

The following diagram indicates the probable feeling experienced with the depression of each Phase type, as a final result of not getting the psychological need met:

Phase	Cellar depression with feeling:
Thinker	Worthless [negative Recognition of Work]
Believer	Hopeless [negative Recognition of Conviction]
Funster	Helpless [negative Contact]
Doer	Abandoned [negative Incidence]
Feeler	Unloved [negative Recognition of Person]
Dreamer	Unwanted [negative Solitude]

Prolonged time spent in the cellar is usually an indication that the person needs medication. A knowledge of Personality Structure and the related kind of depression can inform the choice of medication.

Unit Nine
Phase Issues

Resolving issues is most often the reason we Phase in life. In the mid-eighties I discovered the key issue for each Personality Phase through observation and empirical feedback from random samplings of people who had Phased and experienced working through these issues. Each Personality Phase has an accompanying issue, unique to that Phase in determining if a person Phases again or not.

Chapter 1. The Issue Is the Key

Two out of three people in North America experience a Phase change in their lives. Unfortunately, this Phase shift is most often (about 97 percent of the time) the result of long-term, intense distress that the person eventually resolves (works through).

Phasing is the result of a specific life-presenting issue, which when dealt with authentically would result in a healthy, but painful, healing (emotional) response. If this healthy response is repressed or suppressed, distress behavior occurs and continues for an extended period, until the person finally experiences the underlying, healthy response (emotion), which results in a Phase change to the next "floor" in the condominium. It is important to note that the period of experiencing distress behavior must be prolonged in order to lead to a Phase change once the issue is finally dealt with authentically. In most persons, the period of distress associated with a Phase change lasts between six months and two years.

In other words, each Personality Type, current-Phase floor has a potential "Phasing issue" associated with it. This issue is unique to one and only one Phase type. For example, the issue for the Thinker Phase person is loss.

How this person deals, or doesn't deal with his loss, will determine whether he Phases.

If a person with any other Personality Phase has loss in his life, he will not Phase, no matter how he experiences the loss – in a healthy way, or by suppression, or repression. Loss is the potential issue only for Thinker Phase people.

If the Thinker Phase person feels the loss immediately and allows himself to grieve, he will not Phase. If this Thinker Phase person does not allow himself to grieve, but suppresses/represses the sadness instead, then he will be in the process of "Phasing" – a condition of spending inordinate time in Second Degree Distress. This will continue until he resolves the issue and finally feels the underlying sadness, at which time he will Phase to the next floor in his condominium, have new primary psychological needs, a new corresponding Distress Sequence, and a new Phase issue.

This new Phase itself may last a few years or the rest of the person's life. Phasing helps explain many situations in life – divorce, burn-out, mid-life crisis, and why we are the same person throughout life even though our motivations (dreams, aspirations, careers and personal goals) may change.

There is good news and not so good news about Phasing. It's like winning a Maserati, but having to pay the taxes and insurance for it beforehand. The good news is that once a person has experienced the distress behaviors of Phasing and has Phased to the next floor, she has fully incorporated all the positive features of the prior Phase Personality Type, including the ongoing desire to have those needs satisfied positively (although no longer primarily). In fact, the PTMP results for that person thereafter will indicate that the prior Phase Personality Type has a score of 100 – the same as her Base. This does not mean that the person's favorite Channel or Perception (or any other characteristic associated with Base Personality Type) has changed from that associated with the Base. Rather, it means that the person is almost as comfortable experiencing the world on that floor as she is with respect to her Base.

The not so good news is that Phasing is not only stressful for the individual, it is difficult for others as well. Phasing often results in broken relationships and derailed careers.

It is interesting to note that about three out of every one hundred people who have Phased report that they Phased without experiencing the predicted distress behavior. Consistently two reasons are given for this: 1) a spiritual/religious experience occurred; or 2) there was a significant influx of money into the person's life. A small percentage of the population of Phased individuals who did not experience prolonged distress report that it was caused by a near-death experience.

The following diagram shows the Phase issue for each Phase personality.

Personality Phase	Issue[1]
Thinker	Loss
Believer	Fear
Funster	Responsibility

Doer	Bonding
Feeler	Anger
Dreamer	Autonomy

The following chapters describe the Phase issues of each of the Personality Types in detail, along with the behaviors that accompany Phasing. It is important to keep in mind that all of these behaviors are the classic Second Degree Distress behaviors of the Phase Type, which also present when the person does not get his or her Phase needs met positively. It is not the nature of the behavior that indicates Phasing, it is the intensity and duration of the behavior and the fact that getting psychological needs met positively does not terminate the behaviors. In other words, one is driven to resolve the issue by experiencing the Second Degree Distress behaviors of the Phase, not in order to get positive psychological needs, but in order to bring into consciousness the authentic, underlying emotion and to feel it.

Chapter Notes

[1] Kahler, Taibi. T.A.S.P., Taibi Kahler Associates, Inc., 1997.

Chapter 2. When Phase Thinkers Don't Feel Sad

The key to whether a Thinker Phase client will Phase or not is his response to loss. Loss can include not only the death of a loved one, but also any loss about which a person would feel strongly. For example, loss of time, loss of a relationship, loss of an opportunity, loss of a promotion, or loss of a goal.

Let's look at two friends, Jim and Frank. They are both Thinker–Thinker, 23 years-old, and until recently have not had a major loss in their lives to test whether they will Phase or not.

Within the last three months Jim and Frank each had a favorite Aunt who died, a long-time pet dog that died, and each failed to receive a promotion at work that he really wanted.

Jim responds to each loss by suppressing his grief, refusing to feel his sadness. When his Aunt died, he helped with the funeral proceedings but never shed a tear. "I just hope I can live to be 95 like she did."

Very soon Jim's behavior changes. "I thought I was going to explode … like a volcano, and spill all over everybody. I was frustrated almost all the time. I kept thinking of how stupid people were acting: colleagues making mistakes, my wife messing up the check book, my daughter not putting her toys away. Nobody was thinking clearly." The more Jim suppressed his grief, the more he wore his Attacker Mask.

After his dog died, Jim stoically stated: "He was a good dog." No tears, just more frustration. Those around Jim became concerned about his "short fuse" and inordinate amount of anger.

When Jim didn't get the promotion for which he had worked so hard, he came home and picked a fight with his wife. She became more and more concerned about Jim and their marriage.

Jim is Phasing – wearing his Thinker Phase Attacker Mask to avoid feeling his losses. The more he needs to be sad, the more frustratedly angry he becomes. In real life we can only hope that this does not cost him his marriage or his job.

It is important for those around Jim to understand the dynamics involved in his Phasing. The most painful feeling for a Thinker Phase person is sadness. Jim is avoiding this pain – but it is vital for his well-being and "won't go away." Unconsciously for Jim, his Attacker Mask is justifiable: "I have to yell at you to get your attention so that you will think clearly. If you do not think clearly, then something bad will happen to you. If something bad happens to you, I will have to feel my sadness at losing you. I'd rather feel angry at you than feel that pain."

We can often tell that a person is Phasing by observing their behavior. Jim takes his five-year old daughter to the park. He sees an old friend and goes over to talk with him. In the meantime, his daughter has dropped her ball, and it has rolled into the street. She goes after it. A truck is coming. She doesn't see the truck.

Jim sees his daughter and races toward her. At the last second he pulls her from in front of the passing truck. Shaking her, he yells: "Are you stupid!?" "How many times…" And the Attacker Mask tirade continues, sometimes punctuated with a slap "to make sure she understands how important it is to think clearly."

When someone is Phasing, they often are *compelled* to do things that they normally wouldn't do. They stay in their basement of distress more often and more intensely. Offering the psychological needs of the Phase is seldom palliative because behind the Second Degree mask of a Phasing person is the unfelt authentic emotion, not unmet psychological needs.

A Process Therapist would focus on helping Jim grieve. Once Jim felt his sadness, he would Phase to his next floor in his condominium, have new psychological needs in his foreground, a new Distress Sequence, and a new potential issue, all related to that floor Phase.

What about Frank? He too had losses.

When Frank's Aunt died, he helped with the funeral proceedings and then grieved for her. We saw no unusual display of his Attacker Mask, as he had no need to use it to cover up sadness. He felt his sadness.

When his dog died, he buried him under the tree that they had so often visited while hunting together. And he spent the night with his good friend, crying, and saying goodbye.

When he didn't get the promotion, he looked at his wife with tears in his eyes and said, "I worked as hard as I could. I didn't get the promotion. I'm really sad." And he cried in front of her, and they were closer.

One day Frank took his daughter to the park. He saw an old friend. They started to talk. Frank's daughter dropped her ball. It rolled into the street. A truck was coming.

When Frank grabbed her, it was much different from when Jim grabbed his daughter. Frank has been dealing with his losses by feeling his grief. He has no need to put on an Attacker Mask, as he has been feeling sad with each loss. He says to his daughter, "Thank God you're alive." He does not attack. He does not lecture. He does not hit her. He may give her a Thinker reminder about the rules of not going into the street, but does so in his condominium, not through his Attacker Mask.

Frank *will not* Phase in life. He will remain a Thinker Base in a Thinker Phase forever. He is just where he "needs" to be. All Frank will need to do is to continue to get his Thinker Phase needs met positively in order to stay "balanced." And as he visits all his floors, he can feel "self-actualized."

Several movies are valuable viewing for Phasing Thinkers:

- Dr. Jack MacKee in *The Doctor* Phases from Thinker to Feeler.

- Peter Banning in *Hook* Phases from Thinker to Funster.

- Henry Stanley in *Stanley and Livingston* Phases from Thinker to Believer.

- George in *Same Time, Next Year* Phases from Thinker to Feeler.

- Chuck Noland in *Castaway* Phases from Thinker to Feeler.

Chapter 3. When Phase Feelers Don't Feel Angry

The issue that tests whether or not a Feeler Phase person will Phase is anger. For many people anger has a negative connotation. Anger is one of those emotions that can be positive or negative, depending on how it is experienced and expressed. In and of itself, anger has no "power."

There are four basic kinds of anger, three of which are negative and found in the basement of distress. Distressed Thinkers and Believers hold onto anger and show it through their Attacker Masks. Distressed Funsters and Doers hold onto anger and show it through their Blamer Masks. Distressed Feelers and Dreamers turn anger inward and experience it in their Drooper Masks.

None of these is a healthy, authentic expression of anger. Healthy anger is not held onto. Healthy anger is expressed without attack, blame, or self-recrimination. No Myths of "make feel bad" are involved with healthy anger. Healthy anger is expressed without expectations of change. Healthy anger disappears upon expression.

Lawanda, a Feeler-Feeler, has a hard time saying "no" to people. She often over adapts and puts others first. When she is around people who are angry, she feels something is wrong. She "cannot" bring herself to tell people that she is angry at them. Lawanda is Phasing.

I believe healthy anger is the second most precious verbal gift we can give a loved one. The first is expressing love.

Why? If we express healthy anger without attack, blame, or self-recrimination, then the anger is "out," "gone"– no longer held onto. Retained anger is expressed through Attacker, Blamer, or Drooper Masks. None of these masks involve or encourage intimacy. Therefore, couples who hold onto anger through these masks cannot maintain a long-term, intimate relationship.

Healthy anger is a gift because it is expressed and released, and therefore not used to sabotage intimacy at a later time through the masks. A healthy offer of anger is without attack, blame, manipulation, or expectation of change. A healthy acceptance of anger is appreciation of the sharing, without feeling hurt, attacked, blamed, or manipulated, which would have led to holding onto anger for a counter-attack, blame, or self-recrimination.

There is a simple marriage counseling technique that teaches how to share healthy anger. A couple sits facing one-another. One person starts by saying "I am angry about ____." After each such statement, the other person says, "I heard you say you were angry ____," and fills in what was said. This requires being in the condominium, and not in his own basement "taking it personally or reloading." And the person is to continue with, "Thank you." Again, the "Thank you" is for letting out the anger, rather than holding onto it.[*]

After several of these, the roles are reversed. As a final closure, the same design is used with replacing, "I'm angry ____," with "What I love about you is ____."

Phasing Feelers do not express their anger, believing that "it will hurt someone's feelings" or it will result in their being rejected. Consequently they will likely continue to invite and be rejected until they allow the authentic anger to be expressed.

Several movies are valuable viewing for Phasing Feelers:

- Doris in **Same Time, Next Year** Phases from Feeler to Rebel.

- George in **Phenomenon** Phases from Feeler to Thinker.

- Jing-mei in **Joy Luck Club** Phases from Feeler to Believer.

---

[*] Any signs of basement distress are unacceptable, as they would constitute holding onto anger.

Chapter 4. When Phase Believers Don't Feel Afraid

Fear is the issue for a Believer Phase person. Specifically, it is the fear that he will not be perfectly competent in a new position of responsibility involving others.

Life can present this issue both personally and professionally. In personal life, this issue is often tested with parenthood. "I didn't take a course in 'How to be a parent'." Or, later in life tested with taking care of one's own parent(s), when they cannot function for themselves.

Juan and Julia married earlier than most of their friends. Julia had a baby and had to quit her job at the floral shop, where she had become quite proficient in creating center pieces and silk flower arrangements. She was overjoyed to be a new mother and as a Feeler loved to hold, smell, and nurture her baby girl.

Juan, a Believer-Believer, was a conscientious employee at American Bank and Trust and believed he had a promising future in the banking business. He, too, was a proud parent, yet found himself tense around the baby. His shoulders and neck seemed to hurt constantly.

At first he believed his noticing what was wrong or missing in the nursery was a result of his keen ability to notice things. Yet, he soon became aware that he was drawn to seeing what was missing or wrong not only in the nursery, but everywhere in the house.

He particularly noticed when Julia didn't hold the baby the way she should, or hold the bottle high enough, or wipe the baby's bottom enough times, or burp the baby correctly.

Julia handled Juan's observations without feeling attacked, at first, because they were usually accurate. But then he started to preach at her about how she should be holding the baby and feeding the baby. Then Juan began scolding her for not picking up the crying baby soon enough, and Julia became very concerned that there was something wrong with Juan.

Juan is Phasing. The more fear he has of not being a perfectly competent parent, the more he will find wrong with how Julia is parenting (Be perfect-P), and the more he will preach at and scold her through his Attacker Mask. He will continue this behavior until he becomes aware of this fear and faces it in a healthy way, at which time he will Phase to his next floor.

At the bank Juan also is experiencing distress. He has recently been promoted to Assistant Branch Manager, with supervisory responsibilities for several employees. As a Believer he has always been observant, and it has served him well. Now, that same ability seems to work against him. He naturally is drawn to see anything out of place and focus on it.

Juan feels frustrated that people around him do not seem to be as dedicated as he is. Many times a day he wants to lecture them with a reprimand about their lack of loyalty to their profession: "You should be just as conscientious with a customer whose savings is $100 as one whose savings is $100,000."

Juan's frustration level increases daily, and he finds himself blurting out scolding remarks to his subordinates.

He is Phasing and will need to deal with his fear of not being perfectly competent in parenting and supervising before it costs him too much.

A movie that is valuable viewing for Phasing Believers:

- Lieutenant Dan Taylor in *Forrest Gump* Phases from Believer to Thinker.

Chapter 5. When Phase Funsters Don't Feel Sorry

There is authentic "sorry" and cover-up "sorry." When your Funster cousin Melvin spills Merlot on your Kuba kilim rug, and flashes a Cheshire cat smile with a "Geez, I'm so sorry" grin, he's not being authentic.

Genuine apologies with remorse from a Funster are hard to give, and a pleasure to receive, as they connote taking responsibility for the action and often for the emotion.

"It's not my fault! Nobody told me it was due today." whines Chas, a Funster-Funster. Lately it seems that he has more energy in defending that he has no responsibility when things go wrong, than he has for dealing with them.

This pattern seems to have spilled over into other problem solving areas as well. Instead of putting energy into a solution, Chas puts energy into telling others why their proposed suggestions won't work. His watchword phrase has become "Yes but …."

Several months ago Chas was hired on his first job out of college. At first he liked it because it gave him an opportunity to be on his own from his parents, who had helped finance a long and difficult time at several schools. Having a knack for art, he finally had gotten a degree in Landscape Architecture.

After just a week he decided that he didn't like working with "so many robots," but he knew that he couldn't get another job right away and had already spent his graduation monies on a new laptop.

Chas had always felt cornered in life, but this time he knew that his parents would not help him financially. And, as he thought about it, he realized that he had even promised to start paying them back out of his monthly paycheck.

"Bummer!" he muttered to himself. "If they hadn't made me promise to pay them back right away, I wouldn't be in this mess."

The more he blames, the angrier he gets. The angrier he gets, the more he blames.

In Maslow's terminology, Chas is challenging himself with physiological and safety needs. In PTM terminology he is avoiding having to take physical and emotional responsibilities by wearing his Blamer Mask. He is Phasing.

Several movies are valuable viewing for Phasing Funsters:

- Daniel Hiliard in **Mrs. Doubtfire** Phases from Funster to Feeler.

- Pete Sandrich in **Always** Phases from Funster to Feeler.

Chapter 6. When Phase Dreamers Don't Feel Potent

Essie, a Dreamer-Dreamer, had spent forty-five years of her life with the same routine. When the roosters crowed, her faithful dog Teddy would nudge her until she awoke. By the time Essie had pulled on her weather-worn, flower-sack dress and washed her hands and face, her mother Martha would have their breakfast of fresh eggs, ham, and biscuits ready on the sideboard. They would talk of the day's chores.

After eating, Essie would feed the chickens, slop the hogs, and milk the cows. Then she would collect the eggs and clean out the chicken coops. After that she would let the cows out to pasture, wash down the stalls in the barn, and throw down several bales of hay from the loft. By that time lunch was ready. And they would often eat in silence.

After eating, Essie would clean the house, tend the garden, and work in the fields. By that time dinner was ready. And they would talk of tomorrow's chores.

After eating, Essie would "shoo" in the chickens from the barnyard, bell in the cows from the fields, and "sooie" in the pigs from the pen. After cooping up the chickens, milking the cows, and again slopping the hogs, she would prepare for bed.

Now it was her time with Teddy, and they would look silently and knowingly at each other until each fell asleep.

In the forty-sixth year of her life, her world changed. Martha died, and the farmhouse was half destroyed by a Spring tornado.

Essie had never felt important. It seemed the only decision she ever had to make before was what dress to wear. She only had five, and one was kept for funerals.

And now there was so much to decide: what to do about the house, what to plant this year, when to sell the livestock, what the arrangements are with the bank, where the tax records are, what did the lawyer mean about having to get the will probated ....

She sat on the porch swing with Teddy. They let the day go and the night come. Teddy nudged her awake, and Essie realized she was in bed, and it was morning. She pulled on her weather-worn, flower-sack dress and fed the chickens, slopped the hogs, and milked the cows, and sat on the porch with Teddy.

The more time she spent in her Drooper, the more insignificant she felt. Essie made no repairs on the house, made no planting plans, kept the livestock she had, ignored the letters from the bank, didn't look for the tax records, and forgot about the lawyer. She couldn't make the important decisions. Life had changed from color to black and white. But after eating, she always knew what to do.

Essie was a Phasing Dreamer.

A valuable movie to view for Phasing Dreamers is:

- Forrest Gump in *Forrest Gump* Phases from Dreamer to Feeler.

Chapter 7. When Phase Doers Don't Feel Intimate

Caesar was a young politician who had just been elected to the Parliament after years in local politics. In his past, Caesar had Phased from his Believer Base to Thinker and later to his current Doer Phase. As one would expect, this was a stimulating time in Caesar's career, as he experienced the world of national politics and the whirl of life in the capital. Fueled by new energy to action, he strove to be one of the first, as he jested, "ignobles" to rise in his party's hierarchy. And he was.

At a benefit at which he was the keynote speaker, Caesar met Rhoda, and was immediately smitten with her conscientiousness, intellect, and charm. After all, hers was among the oldest and most prominent families in the capital.

Their relationship was made in a vow of dedication to one-another's success, a singularity of purpose, and a mission to enhance the quality of life for each citizen. They also respected and liked each other. He wanted to be Prime Minister, and she wanted it too. They held their futures in their hands.

Before he was fifty, Caesar reached his goal as he was elected the leader of his party and they then won a Parliamentary majority – he was Prime Minister. It was the most exciting time in his life.

According to PTM, Caesar had it all. His primary Doer Phase need for excitement was frequently met by media events, social soirees, and shindigs with international celebrities.

Caesar had veni, vidi, vici'd. As the leader of his country, he could easily get met his Base Believer needs of Recognition of Work and Recognition of Conviction as he helped enhance the quality of life on a daily basis for all in his country.

But the issue of bonding was rising in Caesar.

He didn't drink to excess. He didn't do drugs. He didn't gamble. How could his unconscious mind test the unresolved bonding issue? How more profound for a Believer Base–Doer Phasing dedicated Prime Minister and committed husband than to test if he will be abandoned by both and all.

Caesar started having an affair, all the time believing it was wrong. He was a good man, an outstanding leader, and devoted to his wife. He knew it could cost him his career and his marriage. Yet, he was driven to resolve the issue.

When a person is Phasing, he is driven to experience the Second Degree Distress behaviors of the Phase, even knowing they may be inappropriate. This is when good people sometimes do bad things.

Star Trek fans are familiar with the episode dealing with "pon farr." When in "pon farr," the mating phase, Vulcans could not control their own actions. Even super bright, self-controlled, logical Spock could not stop his raging attacks on his best friend Captain James Kirk while in this phase.

Doer Phasing people do things to abandon others for fear of being abandoned again. If those others neither allow themselves to be abandoned, nor abandon the Phasing Doer, but rather forgive and accept the person, then he will Phase, experiencing this acceptance as a form of intimacy. The "testing" is complete, with bonding rather than abandonment.

In his country, Caesar was chastised by his peers, but allowed to remain a valued member of Parliament after his term as Prime Minister ended.

His wife forgave him as well, and Caesar Phased to his next floor, which was Feeler, with the new psychological motivations of caring about people and relationships.

With love in his heart for Rhoda, Caesar rededicated his life to the rights of the individual and became the most beloved ombudsman in his country. Historians would record these good deeds of the leader, not the misdeeds of a man.

Valuable movies to view for Phasing Doers:

- Jonas Nightengale in *Leap of Faith* Phases from Doer to Feeler.

- Bob Merrick in *Magnificent Obsession* Phases from Doer to Believer.

- Zack Mayo in *An Officer and a Gentleman* Phases from Doer to Believer.

- Lt. Col. Jack Slade in *Scent of a Woman* Phases from Doer to Believer.

Chapter 8. Phase Cover-up and Authentic Emotions

The following diagram gives the Phase, the cover-up, and the authentic emotions.[1]

	Emotions	
Personality Phase	**Cover-up**	**Authentic**
Thinker	Frustratedly Angry	Sad
Believer	Righteously Angry	Afraid
Funster	Vengeful	Sorry

Doer	Vindictive	Intimate
Feeler	Sad	Angry
Dreamer	Insignificant	Potent

The most painful emotion for a person to experience while Phasing is the authentic one associated with that Phase issue. The most "justifiable" emotion is the cover-up feeling.

Chapter Notes

[1] Kahler, Taibi. "Process Therapy Model," Taibi Kahler Associates, Inc., 2004.

Unit Ten
Treating Scripts

A client's Script becomes a problem the more time he spends in Second Degree Distress.

Chapter 1. Scripts with the Therapist

Knowing the client's Script will provide the therapist with valuable information about how the client may go about sabotaging her life, as well as the therapy process.

After Script

Feeler clients with this Script over adapt to therapists, and in so doing sabotage treatment. Their experience is, "I had a feeling this wouldn't work. I felt the therapist really didn't like me."

Until Script

Thinker and Believer clients with this Script put off doing new, therapy-suggested behaviors until they can be assured of doing it perfectly.

Always Script

The Funster who plays out her Script in therapy leaves, blaming the therapist who wouldn't rescue. The Doer who plays out the Script in treatment also leaves, "cornering" the therapist with manipulations of non-payment, lies, threats of harassment claims, etc.

Never Script

Dreamer clients with this Script may never finalize a new therapy decision into action.

Almost I Script

Clients who have this Script almost get what they want most from therapy. If the client is a Funster in a Feeler Phase, he leaves therapy with, "It's my fault." If the client is a Feeler in a Funster Phase, she leaves treatment with, "It's the therapist's fault."

Almost II (professional)

Clients with this Script will appear to have gotten what they wanted in treatment but do not generalize and incorporate it into their professional life.

Almost II (personal)

Clients with this Script need to deal with either or both, "Don't enjoy" or "Don't have fun," depending on their Phase and personality condominium order. They will fail to deal with the injunction and continue to play the martyr in their relationships.

Chapter 2. Negative Psychological Needs.

In the seventies when I first discovered that the Scripts were generated by the Drivers at First Degree, I naively suggested dealing with them just by making a thinking decision.

For example, as I presented at the Huron Valley Institute (circa 1975), and as referenced in *The Total Handbook of*

Transactional Analysis, by Brown and Woollams, 1977[1] (*See* Appendix A-2):

<u>Until</u>   1) Do the work now with client, not later; 2) Keep work short; OK to work before it's all figured.

<u>After</u>   1) Give permission and get contract not to use work to invite bad feelings later; 2) Stroke after positive statements; 3) End work on positive note.

<u>Always</u>   1) No hedging or disowning: OK to make decisions, OK to make commitments, OK to state feelings, thoughts, and opinions; 2) Encourage and stroke risk taking–OK to make mistakes, change mind.

<u>Never</u>   1) Stroke each step toward OK'ness, no matter how small; 2) Confront by inviting into Adult; 3) Stroke Free Child freely.

<u>Almost</u>   1) Finish the work; 2) Finish each sentence.

But the key in dealing with Scripts is to stay out of Second Degree Distress. The most common reason a person experiences Second Degree Distress is that she is "settling for" getting her Phase needs met negatively, when those same Phase psychological needs were not met positively.

Therefore, the best treatment for the Script is simply to get the psychological needs of the Phase met positively on a daily and weekly basis.

Chapter Notes

[1] Woollams, Stan and Michael Brown. *TA: The Total Handbook of Transactional Analysis,* Prentice-Hall, Englewood Cliffs, 1977.

Chapter 3. Phasing

The second most common reason that a person spends time in the basement of distress is because he is not dealing authentically with the Phase issue and is Phasing.

Since this is the time that a person stays longer and more intensely in Second Degree Distress, it is the time of greatest risk for a person to "play out" his Script.

The best treatment for dealing with the Script at this time is to help the client resolve the Phase issue by experiencing the underlying authentic emotion.   Getting Phase psychological needs met positively can ameliorate but not satiate Phasing.

Chapter 4. Individualized Client Homework

The PTMP report identifies for the client her Phase psychological need(s) and provides Homework for getting these needs met regularly. The following is such an example for Believer Phase clients:[1]

Homework Plan

It is important for you to lead a life consistent with your beliefs, values, and opinions. Whenever possible you like to exercise your influence, impacting upon the growth and direction of others. You need to be around others who share your high standards of integrity, dependability, and trust. For example, you could meet your RECOGNITION OF CONVICTION needs in the following ways:

- Each day prioritize what I believe will be the best investment of my time to ensure quality expenditure of effort.
- Reaffirm daily to myself the value of my accomplishments even before I review my "to do" lists.
- Make agendas for my meetings.
- Reward myself for dedicated service.
- Earn and display one or more awards or pictures with people whom I respect for accomplishing something I believed in doing well.
- Review the mission statement to be sure that goals and objectives are consistent.
- Share my work with others and enjoy their positive feedback on the quality of my labors.
- Join a civic group.
- Become active in my religious institution.
- Make suggestions to appropriate persons regarding my ideas for the organization's improvement.
- Organize an office charitable contribution campaign, or get involved in an existing one.
- Speak to local school groups about professional issues or business ethics.
- Involve myself with quality control projects.
- Write a business article about good business principles or ethics.

Chapter Notes

[1] Kahler, Taibi. "T.A.S.P.," Taibi Kahler Associates, Inc., 1997.

Unit Eleven
Phase vs. Base Distress

Phase distress indicates either that psychological needs are not being met positively or that the client is Phasing. Base distress (in a client who has already Phased one or more times) indicates that the client is re-experiencing the cover-up feeling of the resurfacing Base issue, rather than dealing with it by experiencing the authentic feeling.

Chapter 1. Am I Phasing?

Subjectively, a person is aware of Phasing when he is "living in the basement of distress" and can't seem to do anything about it. Whatever the Phase distress behavior has been in the past, it is unrivaled by the intensity and frequency of the same behavior while Phasing. Whatever the issue is, it becomes directly related to the amount of time in this basement behavior.[*]

For example, if the issue is loss, then every small, missed, ungrieved opportunity intensifies the amount of Thinker Phasing Attacker Mask and frustrated anger that the client experiences.

---

[*] Even getting psychological needs met positively does not stop the distressed behavior, though it might provide temporary relief. Colloquially, what's behind the Mask is not unmet needs, but unmet issues.

If the issue is anger and it is not felt authentically, then each time a Feeler Phasing client has not asserted herself in an important decision or when she was upset with someone, the more she will feel sad through her Drooper Mask, and the more mistakes she will make.

The more a Believer Phasing client must make new, important decisions that affect subordinates, family members or others for whom he is responsible, the more often he will push his beliefs with righteous anger through his Attack Mask as he does not deal with his fear of not being perfectly competent.

The more a Funster Phasing client is expected to be responsible for her actions, the more likely she is to blame, become vengeful and claim to be blameless, not yet having something to replace believing in the Myths.

The more a Doer Phasing client is given the opportunity of emotional closeness, the more likely he will manipulate the giver, having not yet dealt with the issue of intimacy.

The more a Dreamer Phasing client must make an important decision, the more likely she is to shut down, having not yet dealt with the issue of autonomy.

The less the authentic feeling of the issue is experienced, the more the masked behaviors of the Phase continue.

Chapter 2. Has an Old Issue Resurfaced from Base or Stage?

When a person starts to experience and show the behavior of a Distress Sequence of a Personality Type other than of the Phase, then it is likely that an old issue has surfaced again and is not being dealt with in a healthy way. This could be of the Base or of a Stage – an experienced Phase other than the Base or current Phase. It will not be the Distress Sequence of a Personality Type that has not yet been a Phase.

The basement distressed behavior will identify for the therapist which personality Phase is involved, which in turn will pinpoint the issue to address in treatment.

Claudette is a Thinker Base, Stage Funster, in a Feeler Phase. She is a motivational speaker and has committed to a week of seminars abroad in France.

She lives alone, except for her two "babies," Bitte and Danke. Claudette has hired a house-sitter, plant sitter, and "baby" sitter for these two Dachshunds.

Like most Thinkers, Claudette has a great capacity to anticipate problems.[*] She has already provided for her babies by having a doggie door that connects the back yard and the garage, which is temperature controlled.

As an extra precaution she buys a lock for the fenced-in back yard gate, thinking, "Now no one can open the gate and let my babies out to get hurt." And she takes the keys with her to France.

On the second day of her seminar Claudette receives a message that her only niece has died. However, she decides to stay and fulfill her commitment, missing the funeral and putting the death out of her mind as best she can.

She arrives home several days later only to find the gate wide open. Bursting through the front door, Claudette

---

[*]   This is due to the Thinker's need for predictability to forestall potential losses.

screams at the sitter, "Who was the stupid idiot who opened the gate! What have you done to my babies!"

Informatively the sitter responds, "Oh ma'am, Bitte and Danke are fine. They're in the back bedroom. There was a gas leak, and the gas company had to get into the backyard. We looked everywhere for the keys to the lock. They had to cut it off."

Clearly Claudette's behavior did not come from her Feeler Phase, but from her Thinker Attacker Mask. And her attack had nothing to do with the dogs, but rather her Base Thinker issue of loss. That night she dreamed that her babies were lost. She couldn't find them, no matter how long she searched.

The next morning Claudette took a plane to Chicago, went to the cemetery where her niece was buried, and grieved. She no longer wore her Thinker Attacker Mask.

Although we finally 'deal" with an issue in Phasing, if life again presents that same issue, we must again deal with it. If we do not, we get fixated in the related Phase basement.[*]

The good news is that most people, most of the time, are able to deal with previously experienced Phase issues in an authentic way immediately and thereby avoid the related distress.

---

[*] We are looking at our data to see if experiencing this Base (or even Stage) basement of distress may be harder on a person emotionally and physically.

Chapter 3. Will I Phase Again?

Whatever your current Phase is, it has a potential issue with it.

If life has presented that issue to you in a significant way, and you allowed yourself to feel the authentic emotion in response, then you are not likely to Phase again.

If life has presented that issue to you in a significant way, and you have not allowed yourself to feel the authentic emotion, but rather the cover-up one, then you are probably Phasing.

If life has not presented that issue to you in a significant way yet, then at least you can be aware of the importance of the personality dynamics involved.

Unit Twelve
Issues in Therapy

PTM identifies the core issue for each Personality Type. When the client is avoiding the authentic feeling, two degrees of justification occur: at the Driver level as a defense mechanism and in the basement as a failure mechanism. Decisions to stop performing the Driver behavior or to stop the failure mechanism don't deal with the underlying issue. The client resolves this issue by the therapist helping him to deal with the authentic emotion.

Chapter 1. How Thinkers Defend Against Loss

PTM posits that the driving force central to each Personality Type is the Perception and to each Personality Phase is the issue.

The Phase Thinker's issue is loss. When the client is avoiding the authentic feeling of being sad, two degrees of justification occur: 1) at the Driver level, the connection is, "I'll Be perfect and do the thinking for you so that you won't get hurt."; 2) in the basement, "I'll tell you how stupid you are so that you will think clearly." A decision to stop doing the thinking for you, or to stop over controlling, doesn't deal with the underlying issue of loss. The client resolves this issue by the therapist helping him or her to feel sad.

Chapter 2. How Feelers Defend Against Anger

The Phase Feeler's issue is anger. When the client is avoiding the authentic feeling of being angry, two degrees of justification occur: 1) at the Driver level, the connection is, "I'll Please you and over adapt so that you won't reject me."; 2) in the basement, "I'll put myself down and do things wrong to get your attention." A decision to stop over adapting, or to stop making mistakes, doesn't deal with the underlying issue of anger. The client resolves this issue by the therapist helping him or her feel angry.

Chapter 3. How Believers Defend Against Fear

The Phase Believer's issue is fear (of not being perfectly competent when responsible for others). When the client is avoiding the authentic feeling of being afraid, two degrees of justification occur: 1) at the Driver level, the connection is, "I'll expect you to Be perfect and point out your imperfections so that you won't fail."; 2) in the basement, "I'll preach at you to scare you into believing how important what I'm telling you is." A decision to stop pointing out your shortcomings, or to stop pushing my beliefs, doesn't deal with the underlying issue of fear. The client resolves this issue by the therapist helping him or her feel afraid (of not being perfectly competent when responsible for others).

Chapter 4.   How Dreamers Defend Against Autonomy.

The Phase Dreamer's issue is autonomy. When the client is avoiding the authentic feeling of being potent, two degrees of justification occur: 1) at the Driver level, the connection is, "I'll Be strong and not think or feel for myself so that you won't expect me to make decisions."; 2) in the basement, "I'll shut down or withdraw, so that you will have to tell me what to do." A decision to stop denying that I can think or feel, or to stop passively waiting, doesn't deal with the underlying issue of autonomy. The client resolves this issue by the therapist helping him or her feel potent and make important decisions.

Chapter 5. How Funsters Defend Against Responsibility

The Phase Funster's issue is responsibility (for one's emotions and actions). When the client is avoiding the authentic feeling of being sorry, two degrees of justification occur: 1) at the Driver level, the connection is, "I'll Try hard so that you will do the thinking for me and not hold me accountable."; 2) in the basement, "I'll be blameless so that it's never my fault." A decision to stop inviting others to think for me or to stop blaming, doesn't deal with the underlying issue of responsibility. The client resolves this issue by the therapist helping him to feel sorry, by taking responsibility for his emotions and actions.

Chapter 6. How Doers Defend Against Bonding

The Phase Doer's issue is bonding. When the client is avoiding the authentic feeling of being intimate, two degrees of justification occur: 1) at the Driver level, the connection is, "I'll expect you to Be strong and fend for yourself so that you will not depend on me."; 2) in the basement, "I'll redefine the rules of engagement to push you away before you can abandon me." A decision to stop inviting others to do it all on their own or to stop manipulating, doesn't deal with the underlying issue of bonding. The client resolves this issue by the therapist helping him or her to feel intimate by cultivating and sustaining close relationships.

Unit Thirteen
Personality Development

Personality structure consists of six Personality Types, the order of which is set by about age seven. We are likely born with the first floor "Base" Personality Type, while the order of floors two through six are determined by parenting and the environment, interacting with basic Perceptual temperament.

Chapter 1. Developmental Stages and Personality Structure

Although we are likely born with a Base Personality Type, the ordering of the other five floors is influenced environmentally, mostly from interactions with our caretakers.

In order to understand how this occurs, a closer look at the Phase issues in relation to personality development is warranted. Autonomy and Bonding are related to infancy; Fear and Loss to toddlerhood; and Responsibility and Anger to preschool.

Dr. Erik Erickson postulated developmental stages, with related issues and tasks.[1] If the individual's physical and emotional needs are met sufficiently, that stage "task" is completed. If a person is stymied in the task completion, he will carry the remnants of that task into life.

This is consistent with the presence of PTM Phasing issues later in life and the reason a person "moves" to the next floor after resolving the issue.

I propose the following developmental stages (the "Developmental Stages") and associated Personality Types, issues and ages.[*]

Phase	Issue	Age	Developmental Stage
Dreamer	Autonomy	Early Infancy (0-9 mos.)	Dependence
Doer	Bonding	Late Infancy (9-18 mos.)	Connection
Believer	Fear	Early Toddlerhood (18-24 mos.)	Trust
Thinker	Loss	Late Toddlerhood (24-36 mos.)	Solution
Funster	Responsibility	Early Preschool (36-48 mos.)	Independence
Feeler	Anger	Late Preschool (48-60 mos.)	Relationship

I believe that in each of the Developmental Stages, a child is presented with the opportunity to deal with and incorporate the issue that is associated with the applicable Personality Type. If the person is prevented from dealing with the issue

---

[*] The time frames are approximates.

in an authentic and healthy way, he fails to incorporate the issue and fails successfully to complete the Developmental Stage. This sets up the potential for him to Phase later in life, if he ends up having a Phase Personality Type that is the one associated with the unincorporated issue and unsuccessfully completed Developmental Stage.

Chapter Notes

[1] Erickson, Eric. *Childhood and Society,* Norton, New York, 1964.

Chapter 2. Why Do People Phase?

We have identified how people Phase and how to identify a Phasing client. I believe that the reason someone Phases is that the person is tested in life by an unincorporated issue from the first five years of life, as related to the various Developmental Stages.

When parents and/or significant others do not provide permission for the child to deal with any one of the Personality Type specific issues by doing, showing, or saying what is authentic and healthy, that particular issue is unfinished and susceptible to being "retested" later in life. To paraphrase Dr. Berne:

> Parents of the world: If your children grow up, and
> have problems, don't feel guilty. You probably did
> the best you could at the time. If your children grow
> up, and have no problems, don't take all the credit.

I believe we are born with our Base Personality Type and an ordering of our Perceptions for floors two through six. This "natural" ordering of the higher floors, however, is subject to the natural order of perceptions, the personality structures and dynamics of parents (the "scripting" of caretakers), as well as many other factors that may be situation specific: a sibling for whom to be responsible, death, divorce, disasters, war, etc.

For each person, the first "test" of Phasing will be with respect to the issue of their Base Personality Type. How well did the individual incorporate that issue and complete the associated Developmental Stage? Did the parents provide what was necessary in doing, showing, or saying what is authentic?

Successive potential Phase "tests" are determined by the individual ordering of floors two through six.

If a person Phases, she will have her next floor Phase issue come into prominence, to be "tested" by her life experiences. Whether or not she "passes" the test and remains in that Phase for the remainder of her life, or goes through the Phasing process again, will depend upon whether she successfully completed the corresponding Developmental Stage and incorporated the associated issue.

Chapter 3. Infancy: Dreamers and Doers

I believe the six Personality Type Phasings relate developmentally to the unsuccessful completion of the original Developmental Stages.

I make no reference to a specific "Separation stage." Perhaps the most important element in the emotional development of a child is for the parents to help him separate from physical dependency to emotional independency: protecting the child physically and emotionally until the child has the ability and permission to protect himself emotionally and physically. This separation is incomplete when the individual still believes the four Myths.

Dependence Stage
Early Infancy (Birth to 9 months)

Phase: **Dreamer**

Issue: **Autonomy**

Incorporating feeling: **Potency**

Existential question: **"Am I wanted?"**

Infant autonomy is the awareness of self-directive behavior. Successfully completing this Developmental Stage begins with the reliability of caretakers attending to and meeting the physical and emotional needs of the infant. Such protection and attention allows the infant the opportunity to experience the results of interacting with the environment. This begins the formulation of decisional cause and effect, which incorporates the feeling of potency.

Later in life, an individual in a Dreamer Phase who has successfully completed this Dependence stage will be able to make important, significant personal decisions in life.

Although able to make these kinds of decisions, this individual will have Solitude needs and still will prefer to be externally motivated in mundane situations and well defined expectations and specified parameters of authority. These things provide the Dreamer Phase person with the answer to "Am I wanted?" Time to reflect and "just be" is a battery charge to this Phase type.

Unsuccessful completion of this Dependence stage for an infant can be attributed to unreliability, neglect, or discounting of the infant's basic needs. For example, a continuing pattern of not meeting the infant's basic physical needs such as feeding, changing diapers or holding. Attitudes that could contribute to this pattern could include: "Don't pick up crying babies, you'll spoil them."; "Holding babies just get them overly attached to their mother."; and "All babies cry, just learn to ignore it."

Other circumstances that could result in a failure to incorporate this Dreamer Phase issue include mothers with post partum depression, or those with many other children, needy themselves and too young to help her.

Later in life the Dreamer Phase individual will test this autonomy issue when life requires that a major decision be made. Given this opportunity to be potent and make the important decision, this Dreamer Phase person will likely cope by denying the ability to think or feel (First Degree: Be strong) and passively waiting (Second Degree), including withdrawing and avoiding making the major decision. The experience for this person is likely to be, "I need more support to make this decision."

This Phasing person is likely to shut down with negative Solitude, having little energy even to make daily decisions.

In order to Phase, this Dreamer Phase person will need to attach enough to life and the situation to feel potent and make important, autonomous decisions.

Connection Stage
Late Infancy (9 to 18 months)

Phase:	**Doer**
Issue:	**Bonding**
Incorporating feeling:	**Intimacy**
Existential question:	**"Am I alive?"**

Bonding is the formation of the relationship between mother and infant through frequent and consistent physical and emotional contact. Successful incorporation of the bonding issue provides the infant with the incorporated feeling of intimacy.

Later in life, this same bonding issue is the Doer Phase person's basis for defining intimacy. In other words, the adult Doer Phase individual who originally was successful in incorporating this developmental issue of bonding and thereby completing the Connection stage will be open to an intimate relationship.

Furthermore, this individual will have Incidence needs: a drive for a great deal of excitement in a short period of time, adrenalin rushes, and thrills. This provides the Doer Phase person with the answer to the question, "Am I alive?"

A failure to incorporate this Doer Phase issue during the Connection stage is likely the result of physical or emotional abandonment. Many of the Dependence stage parenting deficiencies also can be attributed to the unsuccessful completion of this Developmental Stage. The salient perceptual distinction is the awareness of the infant to the lack or loss of bonding intimacy.

Later in life the Doer Phase individual is likely to "test" this bonding issue when given the opportunity to be intimate. This person will cope by expecting others to fend for themselves (First Degree: You Be strong) and by manipulating (Second Degree), including redefining agreements, bending or breaking the rules, or conning, all designed to abandon the other person(s). The justification is "I'll abandon you before you can abandon me."

During Phasing, this person is likely to make poor decisions to get (at least) negative Incidence – financially, physically, or emotionally.

In order to Phase, this person will need to feel and accept the offer of emotional closeness. This means re-examining his justification of "emotional vulnerability," and establishing an intimate "bonding" relationship.

Since this is relational, it requires a great deal from those whom she has manipulated. They need to sidestep the manipulations, not be abandoned, refuse to be victimized, define themselves, and confront the negative behaviors while still giving the message, "I won't abandon you." Having "recreated" the original abandonment experience, the Doer Phasing person can finally complete the Connection stage by finding and experiencing true intimacy, and by Phasing to her next personality condominium floor.

Chapter 4. Toddlerhood: Believers and Thinkers

Trust Stage
Toddlerhood (18 to 36 months)

Phase:	**Believer**
Issue:	**Fear**
Incorporating feeling:	**Afraid**
Existential question:	**"Am I worthy?"**

Trust stage fear is the awareness of and concern about potential harm or danger. Successful completion of this Developmental Stage begins with the caretakers anticipating and attending to the environmental safety needs of the exploring toddler. Such precautions allow the toddler the opportunity to experience the results of interacting with the environment and her fear of the unknown. Almost every new exploratory move, based on "faith," is accompanied by fear. Continued success in judgment increases self-trust, allows appropriate apprehensiveness, and incorporates this Developmental Stage feeling of being afraid. The experience of doing something new should be more rewarding than the fear of doing it.

The adult individual in a Believer Phase who has successfully completed this Trust stage will be aware of and can express when he is afraid. This will be especially important when this person has new responsibilities for other people in his personal or professional life. He can admit, "I am afraid that I am not perfectly competent for this new responsibility." To reinforce this Trust stage, Believer Phase adults have Recognition of Work and Recognition of Conviction as psychological needs. These provide the

Believer Phase person with the answer to the question, "Am I worthy?"

Successful completion of the Trust stage, and the remaining Developmental Stages, require a healthy balance of parenting so that the child has ample opportunities to experience the issue and have her authentic emotion to it reinforced. One of the reasons the game of "Peek-a-boo!" is so good for the child is that it teaches her that she can be afraid, feel it, and then feel happy. She learns that she can be startled, then feel good.

There are several important lessons for the child to be taught. A common toddler fear is that of a vacuum sweeper. "Will it hurt me?" "Will it eat me?"

Unproductive: "Don't be a sissy. Come over here."

Productive: "You were afraid. We are sometimes afraid of things we don't know about. It won't hurt you, just don't touch it unless Mommy is here with you. It picks up little things on the carpet. You are big, so you can't fit inside. I am the one making it do what it does." Gradually help the child deal with any fear of the noise and the movement.

When Attacking anger covers being afraid, help the child realize the underlying authentic feeling.

The new puppy creeps in and startles Jimmy, who is absorbed in his building blocks. He turns and hits the dog with a block. This is a great opportunity for several parenting lessons. Help him understand that he was really feeling scared (under his angry Attack). Tell him what is inappropriate ("We don't hit the puppy"). Let him know what is an appropriate response (You might tell him to say, "No").

When we parents cover our fears by presenting Attacking anger toward our child, we also can use it as a learning experience. "Daddy was angry and yelled at you when you started to pick up the knife. I was really scared that you might get hurt. I'm not really angry at you." And, then the lesson about knives...

Unsuccessful completion of this Developmental Stage is usually the result of the parent(s) either being over protective, or under protective, verbally or behaviorally.

Over protective parental behavior includes not allowing the child to be involved in age appropriate activities: No running, rolling, swinging, riding a tricycle, or climbing. Allowing the child to cling physically to the parent in public or around strangers.

Leaving all the lights on, with the explanation: "So the boogie man won't get you." Staying in the room until the child falls asleep, with the explanation: "So you won't be scared."

Other over protective behaviors are saying frequently, "Don't...!"; constantly cautioning, "Be careful!"; and/or predicting dire consequences, "You'll hurt yourself!" These often invite hesitation or unrealistic fears, discourage exploration, and can be interpreted as attributions of what the child is "expected" to do.

Under protective behaviors can range from ignoring the inquisitive child who puts a key in an unprotected electrical socket, or who finds a can of Drano in the unsecured kitchen cabinet, or who decides to go down the ungated basement stairs, or who wants to play in the water of the unfenced swimming pool, or .... Preparing for the Trust stage requires

205

a great deal of anticipation of the mobile little person's potential activities.

Verbal threats are also counterproductive: "You better listen to me. Do you know what happens to bad little girls? When they're sleeping …."

Many situations involving probable fearful responses can be mediated by acknowledging the child's fear, followed by protection and information. Strangers, animals, doctors, toilets, imaginary creatures, and new situations commonly are scary to children and the mediating response can be planned in advance.

When is play, play? Most little Believers do not find being thrown in the air or twirled a fun experience. They become scared. This can be turned into a positive experience if done in moderation and by confirming that the child smiles or shows other positive signs after each "scary" toss or twirl. Assuming that the child is having fun just because he is screaming may be counter-productive and reinforce more negative fear.[*]

Failing to successfully complete the Trust stage is likely to result in an adult Believer Phase individual denying that he is afraid, especially in such circumstances as becoming a new parent or a new manager, or in any other situation of major responsibility for others. Consequently, this Phase Believer finds imperfections in others (First Degree: You Be perfect) and pushes beliefs (Second Degree), designed to "scare" others into believing as he does.

---

[*] Funsters and Doers, on the other hand, find it fun and exciting.

206

To finalize and incorporate this early stage issue, the Phasing Believer will need to acknowledge not being perfectly competent, and feel the fear of the unknown consequences to himself and others, instead of masking it with righteous anger.

Solution Stage
Toddlerhood (24 to 36 months)

Phase:	**Thinker**
Issue:	**Loss**
Incorporating feeling:	**Sadness**
Existential question:	**"Am I prepared?"**

Solution stage loss results from the failure to succeed in an activity, or in expressing a thought, or in experiencing separation. Continued success in communicating and attaining goals increases the child's confidence sufficiently to deal with losses, resulting in the incorporation of feeling sadness.

The adult individual in a Thinker Phase who has successfully completed the Solution stage will be aware of and can express when he is sad. Losses could include deaths, unmet goals, or any desire unattained. To reinforce the Solution stage, adult Thinkers have Recognition of Work and Time Structure as psychological needs. These provide the Thinker Phase person with the answer to the question, "Am I prepared?"

Successful completion of this stage is the result of parents who encourage thinking, expression, and overcoming of obstacles, to the extent that the child is allowed to fail and to feel her pain of failure or loss – sadness, crying. A parent does this by allowing the child to overcome age appropriate obstacles in order to feel the pleasure of success more than the discomfort of the failures.

Failure to incorporate this Phase issue occurs when the child either continues to feel frustrated with failures, or was not given enough opportunities to fail, and therefore did not test the issue of loss. This also occurs when the child was presented with a loss and his natural sadness (crying) was not permitted.

Unsuccessful completion of this Developmental Stage is likely due to rescuing (over-doing) or prohibiting parents. A common testing situation is when mother leaves the child for the first time with a caretaker. Among the unhelpful things to do are: bribing, begging, discounting the child's sadness ("Big boys don't cry"), or just sneaking off.

Instead, offering empathy acknowledges the child's feeling of sadness, followed by reassuring, "I'll be back." Allowing the child to cry allows a natural closure, as the mother returns later. Interrupting this with over protection risks reinforcing the child's belief that his crying "brought mother back."

Shala is a Feeler single parent, who decides to work in order to help support her toddler son Kirk. As she leaves him for the first time to go to her job, Kirk cries and cries. Shala is distraught and torn in her feelings. She feels responsible for providing income for them both but has a motherly instinct to stay with her child. She believes it is her fault that Kirk feels so sad and internalizes that she must be a bad parent for "making her son feel so bad." Shala is buying into one of the Four Myths.

Shala succumbs to this Myth, and in a distressed Feeler over-doing manner, she decides that she must stay home to "make Kirk feel good." Ironically, this disallows Kirk the opportunity to incorporate the issue.

If Kirk is a Thinker (or ever is in a Thinker Phase), then he will have loss as a Phase test issue. Since the original fixation was with separation loss, Kirk will likely choose someone with whom he will fall in love, knowing unconsciously she will not stay with him, and/or whom he will push away.

A resolution to this issue requires Kirk to accept losses and feel the sadness, which would also result in his Phasing to the next floor in his condominium.

Chapter 5. Preschool: Funsters and Feelers

Independence Stage
Preschool (36 to 48 months)

Phase: **Funster**

Issue: **Responsibility**

Incorporating feeling: **Sorry**

Existential question: **"Am I acceptable?"**

Independence stage responsibility is accepting accountability for both one's actions and one's emotions. Successful completion of this stage begins with social interaction. It also requires an understanding of physical cause and effect, an incorporation of the concept of healthy guilt, and a feeling of responsibility for wrongdoing.

With a healthy parental balance of appropriate reinforcement for positive social behaviors and confrontation and consequences for negative behaviors, the Funster preschooler has the permission to incorporate and express being sorry.

The Funster Phase adult who has successfully incorporated this issue and completed the Independence stage will accept appropriate blame and express regret, as well as accept credit for making herself feel good. To reinforce this Independence stage, Funsters have Contact as their psychological need. This provides the Funster Phase person with the answer to the question, "Am I acceptable?"

First Degree Distress Driver behavior of the Funster is Try hard, which is experienced by the child in Myth terms as, "You're supposed to do the thinking for me to make me feel good."

Second Degree Distress behavior is blaming. The Myth dynamics are likely to be, "You didn't make me feel good enough, so it's your fault that I am feeling bad. I'll just make you feel worse."

So, unsuccessful completion of this stage is the result of parents over-doing and reinforcing the "make feel bad" Myth in the child. This includes not allowing the child to do age appropriate tasks on their own or figuring things out for them that they can figure out themselves.

The key in helping a child take responsibility for his actions and his emotions is to focus on the Myths. How can we expect a child to be responsible for his emotions and ours too? If we can make someone feel good or bad emotionally (the belief of the distressed Funster), then how can we expect a Funster to take responsibility for her own behavior and emotions and be sorry and change?

The Second Degree Distress behavior only ends up reinforcing more negative behavior in the Funster. A common mistake that Thinker and Believer parents make is to threaten Funsters. This is worsened when delivered in Second Degree with frustration. Their very frustration is seen as a payoff by the distressed Funster. "Ha! Ha! I made you feel bad, just like you hurt me." So, parents must first take responsibility for making themselves feel bad and not invite the child to be responsible for their frustration. That's why it is so important for Thinker parents to deal with their own frustrated anger by feeling their underlying sadness. And for Believer parents to deal with their own righteous anger by feeling their underlying fear.

Other self-sabotaging, negatively reinforcing parental comments include, "Why do you embarrass us so?"; "You're driving us crazy!"; "You're breaking your mother's heart."; "Do you realize how many people you are hurting?"; "He does that to make you mad." These reinforce the "make feel bad" Myth.

An incorporation of this issue involves being authentically sorry, which usually is a result of parents no longer over-doing and the Funster child being accepted unconditionally so that he can incorporate sufficient self-love to make himself feel good.

Relationship Stage
Preschool (48 to 60 months)

Phase: **Feeler**

Issue: **Anger**

Incorporating feeling: **Angry**

Existential question: **"Am I loveable?"**

Relationship stage anger is the authentic expression of extreme displeasure at another's behavior, without attack, blame, or self-recrimination. The successful completion of this stage begins with healthy parenting in modeling and accepting anger.

The Feeler Phase person who has successfully incorporated the issue will accept and express anger, knowing it is essential in building intimacy. To reinforce this Relationship stage, Feelers have Recognition of Person and Sensory as their psychological needs. These provide the Feeler Phase person with the answer to the question, "Am I loveable?"

As with all children, successful emotional growth for Feeler children includes being parented through three stages: awareness, expression, and action.[*]

Awareness: A little Feeler comes to her mother jumping up and down, with clinched fists, and screaming.

"Shame on you!" reproves her mother through her Attacker Mask. This little Feeler is not given the awareness of her anger. Thirty years later in treatment when her

---

[*] From a 1973 lecture at the San Diego Institute for Transactional Analysis by Fanita English on "emotion, awareness, expression."

therapist asks her the last time she was angry at her parents, she will likely respond, "I've never been angry at my mother or father in my life." Instead of feeling angry, she feels shame – an intense feeling of guilt but not from what she has done, rather from who she is.

Her treatment will have to include helping her with awareness of her anger.

Parents can help their children with awareness of emotions by connecting the physical behavior to the emotion. To the upset little Feeler say, "You sure are angry." Now she knows that she is feeling angry when she has these physical feelings.

Expression: Another little Feeler yells at her parents, "I hate you! I hate you!" She is clearly aware of her anger.

Through his Attacker Mask, her father warns, "Stop that this minute young lady! You know how that upsets your poor mother. She's depressed enough. Go to your room, and when you can put a smile on your face, and behave yourself, you can come downstairs with us."

This young Feeler is likely to make the following unconscious decision: "My anger can hurt my mother and make her even more depressed. So whenever I get angry, I'll just put on a happy face so that I won't hurt anyone's feelings, and they won't tell me to go to my room (reject me)." This is the Feeler client who cries or laughs when she gets angry. She is having a painful, internal conflict. She's angry with someone, yet responds the same way she decided to decades before. Still believing she can hurt someone's feelings, she "swallows" her anger and internalizes: "I'd rather hurt myself than someone else."

This pattern in life of internalizing anger inevitably results in depression. Furthermore, this victim behavior advertises for, and often gets, persecutors. Yet such Phasing Feelers bemoan, "Why aren't there any good men left?"

A healthy parent response to "I hate you" is "I hear you are very angry at me. I am listening to you. It's OK to tell me that you are angry at me." Follow up with no signs of Drooper, Attacker, or Blamer Masks that would sabotage the permission. Afterwards, continue to show love and acceptance. This will teach the child that expressing the anger with "I'm angry _____" lets it out, no one "got hurt," mom and dad still love me, and I feel better.

Action: A small child has been patiently trailing mother around the grocery store for almost an hour. The checkout line seems unendurably long. The little boy impatiently pulls at mother's dress. "Later. Mother's busy." Still dissatisfied, the little boy tests even further and pinches her.

A useful way of dealing with inappropriate behavior is to tell the child what is unacceptable as well as what is acceptable. As with adults, if we expect a child to give up something negative, there should be something positive to put in its place.

Unsuccessful completion of the Relationship stage results in believing one's anger is so powerful that it can hurt someone's feelings or result in rejection. Consequently, the Feeler Phase person over-adapts (First Degree: Please you) and makes mistakes (Second Degree) to advertise for and receive someone else's attacking anger.

A final incorporation of this issue requires awareness of and expressing of anger without attack, blame, or self-recrimination.

Chapter 6. Chicken or Egg?

Although it appears from observations and personal histories that the unsuccessful completion of a Developmental Stage will be revisited and tested if the person experiences that Phase later in life, the question remains: What determines the order of the personality structure for floors two through six?

Several possible hypotheses can be offered and tested. Among the questions to be considered are: given that we are born with the Base type, does successful completion of a Developmental Stage relegate the associated Personality Type to a higher floor? What is the overall influence of our caretakers on our structure? Does the unsuccessful completion of a Developmental Stage place it lower in one's condominium structure? Is there a degree of unsuccessful completion of Developmental Stages that warrant fixation, which thereby modifies the personality structure above Base and forces the associated Personality Type to become the second floor?

Each of these questions needs to be addressed and researched.

Unit Fourteen

Selecting the Treatment Model to Match the Client's Base and Phase

Whatever the personality structure of the client is, and whatever the choice of treatment modalities, a second-by-second monitoring by the therapist of the process between them is crucial in therapy. Most models devised by leading therapists are a projection of their own personality structure and attract disciples of similar personality Base or Phase. The value, therefore, of many therapy models lies not in their universal – one size fits all – usefulness, but rather in the naturally compatible connection of the personality structures of the disciple therapist treating a matching Base or Phase client.

Chapter 1. Dr. Aaron Beck: Cognitive Therapy (CT)[1]

Cognitive Therapy (CT) began in the 1960s when Dr. Aaron Beck tried to prove that depression was anger turned inward. CT seeks to identify and change "distorted" or "unrealistic" ways of thinking, and therefore to influence emotion and behavior. Clients are taught to notice their moods, then to become aware of the thoughts that accompany them.

CT is thought to come to a close when the client no longer jumps to his old conclusions, but instead considers the evidence logically to find out what is true, and has learned tools to prevent or decrease the severity of relapse.

Base: In Process Therapy terminology, CT would be useful in connecting with Thinker Base individuals or with those who have strong Thinker floors. A simple test of the utility of this CT connection would be if the client kept responding with other Perceptions, or then with First degree Driver distress when CT Asking Channel and Thoughts were consistently offered.

Phasing: PTM contends that a Phasing Thinker would need to be encouraged to feel his or her sadness. Any other Phasing Type would have its own underlying emotion to be addressed. However, a non-Phasing Thinker (Thinker Phase) would likely find value in CT, as it inherently meets the psychological need of Recognition of Work (ideas).

Chapter Notes

[1] Beck, Aaron. Cognitive Therapy and the Emotional Disorders, Meridian, New York, 1967.

Chapter 2. Dr. Carl Rogers: Rogerian Therapy (RT)[1]

Dr. Carl Rogers' theory of person-centered therapy suggests any client can improve without being taught anything specific by the therapist, once he accepts and respects himself.

Dr. Rogers felt that an effective therapist must have three very special qualities: 1) congruence – genuineness and honesty with the client; 2) empathy – the ability to feel what the client feels; and 3) respect – acceptance and unconditional positive regard toward the client.

Base: RT would be the choice model in connecting with Feelers, with offerings from the Comforting Channel plus Emotions, and non-Phasing Feeler Phase clients, who would grow with such Recognition of Person.

Phasing: PTM contends that a Feeler Phasing client's emotion to be encouraged is authentic anger. Any other Phasing type would have its own issue to be addressed. Therefore, an RT therapist who is able to recognize each Phase cover-up feeling, distinguish it from the underlying emotion, and support the authentic one, could be very effective. A caution would be in the initial connecting: five of the six Personality Types do not prefer the Comforting Channel with Emotions.

Chapter Notes

[1] Rogers, C.R. (1959). A theory of therapy, personality and interpersonal relationships, as developed in the client-centered framework. *In S. Koch (ed). Psychology: A Study of science*, at 184-256 (N.Y. McGraw Hill).

Chapter 3.   Dr. Albert Ellis: Rational Emotive Behavior Therapy (REBT)[1]

Dr. Ellis believes that the key to a client's dysfunction is his or her belief system. He maintains that cognitive, emotional, and behavioral problems are a direct result of irrational philosophies and beliefs of the individual.

The role of a REBT therapist is to help the client identify these irrational philosophies that the client believes, show how these beliefs lead to emotional problems, and then teach the client how to change these beliefs, without needing to be accepted or loved.

REBT utilizes expressive-experimental methods and behavioral techniques, not with the intent of helping people emote and feel better, but with the intent of helping them to hold rational beliefs which will result in non-self-defeating behavior.

Base: In a PTM frame of reference it is clear that Dr. Ellis views the world through beliefs. REBT would naturally connect with Believers, but would not likely be successful with several other Personality Types, in particular Feelers. Again, a confirmation of connecting is simple: monitor second-by-second Channels and Perception success or Driver "resistance."

Phasing: If the client is not Phasing, then discussions and clarifications of philosophy and beliefs can meet Believer Phase psychological needs of Recognition of Work and Recognition of Conviction positively. If the client is a Phasing Believer, then PTM contends that feeling the fear is necessary and that it is not sufficient to identify the need to feel it, or the logic of feeling it, or the irrational behavior associated with it. Furthermore, PTM contends that most every Phasing issue does require "emoting in order to feel better."

Chapter Notes

[1] Ellis, Albert and Windy Dryden. *The Practice of Rational Emotive Behavior Therapy,* Springer Publishing Company, New York, 2007.

Chapter 4. Dr. Fritz Perls: Gestalt Therapy (GT)[1]

Gestalt Therapy (GT) was co-founded by Fritz Perls, Laura Perls, and Paul Goodman in the 1940s–1950s. GT emphasizes personal responsibility, and focuses more on process (what is happening) than content (what is being discussed). The emphasis is on what is being done, thought and felt at the moment rather than on what was, might be, could be, or should be.

Therefore, GT is a method of awareness, by which perceiving, feeling, and acting are understood to be separate from interpreting, explaining and judging using old attitudes. The client discovers by her own experience how to become aware of what she is doing psychologically and how she can change it.

A common dynamic to resolve is the "top dog, under dog" parts of the client that do not like one another.

The objective of GT is to enable the client to become creatively alive and to be free from the blocks and unfinished issues that may "diminish optimum satisfaction, fulfillment, and growth."

Base: The student of PTM will have determined that Fritz Perls was a Funster and that his GT is a natural therapy for Funster Base and Phase/Phasing clients. The caution for Funster GT therapists is to process with each client Base type first in her Channel and Perception.

Let's take time to extrapolate. The emphasis of GT is not on the facts of what happened (Cognitive Therapy connection for Thinkers) or the beliefs of what should be (Rational Emotive Behavior Therapy connection for Believers), because

GT does not focus on interpreting, explaining and judging using old data or attitudes.

The emphasis is on personal responsibility. In PTM, that is the issue for Funsters. Clients are to come to their own experiential "aha's" in GT, as is true in life with Funsters, who do not learn from others but must experience on their own.

The "top dog, under dog" technique accomplishes many things for the Funster client. It uses physical movement, which is itself kinesthetically appealing to Funsters. It sidesteps negative transference and "Yes but-ing," while redirecting "blaming" back to the client within his own dialogue. And its inherent Perceptions are Reactions (likes and dislikes).

In an interview with Fritz Perls, Adelaide Bry begins by questioning, "What is Gestalt Therapy?" (Asking Channel with Thoughts). True to the Funster Type, Dr. Perls does not answer in Channel, but rather in his Reactions (likes/dislikes) Perceptual language: "Discussing, talking, explaining is unreal to me. I hate intellectualizing, don't you?" He has made it clear that he is not going to talk about GT, but have her experience it ("Don't you? – like or dislike…") because that is the essence of his model.

Phasing: For Funster Phase/Phasing clients who need to experience and integrate that behind the blaming is the need for self-forgiveness, self-love, and then authentic regret, GT can be a most useful approach. And for each Phasing Personality Type, the GT therapist can facilitate these clients to discover the underlying authentic emotion to closure. To review, for the victim Feeler Phasing client this authentic emotion is anger; for the persecuting Thinker and Believer

Phasing clients these authentic emotions are sadness and fear, respectively; for the victim Dreamer Phasing client this authentic emotion is potency; and for the vindictive Doer Phasing client this authentic emotion is intimacy.

Chapter Notes

[1] Perls, Fritz, and Ralph Hefferline & Paul Goodman. *Gestalt Therapy: Excitement and Growth in Human Personality.* The Gestalt Journal Press, Highland, New York, 1994.

Chapter 5. Dr. Ogden Lindsley: Behavior Therapy (BT)[1]

Behavior Therapy (BT) was coined by Ogden Lindsley and emphasizes that psychological matters can be studied scientifically by observing overt behavior, without discussing internal mental states. All things that organisms do – including acting, thinking and feeling – are regarded as behaviors. Behaviorism takes the position that all theories should have observational correlates but that there are no philosophical differences between publicly observable processes (such as actions) and privately observable processes (such as thinking and feeling).

Base: Dreamer Base clients open to the Directing Channel and Inactions (reflections) might be most open to BT.

Phasing: Dreamer Phase clients could also do well with continued positive reinforcement.

Chapter Notes

[1] Lindsley, Ogden.

Chapter 6. Dr. Martin Groder: Asklepieion Program (AP)[1]

In 1969 Dr. Groder combined Transactional Analysis and the Synanon Game into the Asklepieion Program (AP) at the Marion, Illinois, US maximum security prison. Three basic principles were emphasized in AP: 1) winning for oneself is dependent on others winning too; 2) winning personally is much easier in a society that functions well and has productive participation from all of its members; and 3) thinking and planning is necessary in taking control of one's life.[*]

The Community consisted of a group of convicts committed to straight talk, positive stroke economy, growth and change. Any gross behavior (gambling, carrying weapons, fighting, etc.) was confronted.

An hour a day was devoted to learning Transactional Analysis.

Two hours daily was devoted to the Game. Someone was "indicted" with an accusation, either true of false. The indicted individual must sit in the center and think clearly, not cleverly, in response to high intensity accusations and confrontations by two dozen inmates.[†]

Closure for this person would be evidenced by his being honest, open, and OK. Everyone is involved, both as therapists and client. At the end of the two hours, any "bad

---

[*] All three of these basic principles counter the dynamics of distressed Doers: abandonment, impulsivity, and failure.

[†] An ideal prison environment for getting Doer positive Incidence.

feelings" are expressed and dealt with at that time. Final closure is the appreciation of positive feelings for participants.[*]

Dr. Groder explained to us "visitors" that nothing else that he and others had tried with convicts had been effective. He knew that positive rewards had merit.

Then he explained, "Then I got the picture. Go with the flow." He stood up, moved to the black board, and drew two mountains with a valley in between. Pointing to the valley, he said, "That's Neuroticville, where nine-to-five lunch buckets live. You can't turn the guys here into everyday neurotics."

Again pointing back and forth at the peaks of the two mountains, he continued, "You turn the clever into clear thinking. You turn the con into the entrepreneur. That's how they fit back into society."

PTM research has confirmed Dr. Groder's intuition: Doers need Incidence – a great deal of excitement in a short period of time. A large percentage of convicts are Doer Base or Phase, having committed crimes because of the drive for this Incidence, albeit negatively.

The Game provided positive Incidence. No wonder Dr. Groder was so successful. If Doer convicts are not provided such positive Incidence, they will find a way to get negative Incidence needs met: gambling, carrying weapons, fighting, etc. And by closing the Game with "warm fuzzies,"[2] Dr. Groder reinforced positive bonding and authentic intimacy among the convicts. In fact, the recidivism rate for graduates of the Game was reported to be 12%.[3]

---

[*] This provided intimacy for Phasing Doers.

I spent one Saturday a month, for six months, visiting the prison but not "visiting" the Game. Only one visit to the Community was allowed; thereafter, involvement required participating in the Game, not just observing.

The game is not for the faint of heart. It is a rush to be yelled at by hardcore convicts, just spitting distance from your face.

"You, College. Get in the chair!" My heart started to race, but I put on my smiling, hope-you-like-me face. I was twenty-six, working on my doctorate, and a Thinker–Feeler. In that Feeler Phase, I sure wanted everybody to know I cared about people.

"You're so smart. Tell us what love is."

Trying to impress them, I responded predictably from Base and Phase: "I think love is when you care more about the other person than you do yourself." Pleased with my answer, I waited for their affirmation.

I was quickly jolted out of my self-absorption: "You phony! You're a Rescuer, aren't you! You're one of those patsies that won't confront your friend when he's had too much to drink. You'll talk to him, but you won't just take his keys away! All talk, no action! Phony! Phony! Phony!," they chanted.

And the Game was afoot.... They had quickly and accurately assessed that I had unfinished business with Rescuing, *i.e.*, overly taking care of people. They confronted me and led me to self-awareness and clear thinking about what I would do differently in the future. A very nice piece of therapy by skillful therapists.

I have never felt so close, so soon, to a group of strangers than when I finished, and they told me how they felt about me and the work I had done. Hugging each, I felt intimate with men who were freer in OK'ness than those of us who are prisoners of our own Myths.

Base/Phasing Doer clients could benefit most by such a confrontational type of group therapy, which provided Incidence and caring support.

Chapter Notes

[1] Groder, Martin. "Asklepieion: An Integration of Psychotherapies," *Transactional Analysis After Eric Berne,* Harper and Row, New York 1977.
[2] Steiner, Claude. *Scripts People Live By,* Grove Press, New York 1974.
[3] Loria, Bruce. Personal communication, 2008.

Chapter 7. Gloria

PTM offers a process by which therapists may utilize their techniques and approaches to therapy, in a manner tailored to the individual client. In other words, treatment depends upon the personality structure of the client, not a single model approach in which the therapist may have specialized. The film *Gloria*[1] beautifully demonstrates the importance of process. A young lady is interviewed by Dr. Rogers, Dr. Ellis, and Dr. Perls. They are then asked their assessment of how valuable their approach was. Gloria is then asked how she experienced each session. The results were remarkably predictable, but first let's have a brief review.

It is not uncommon to have a natural bias for a treatment model, even for us therapists. After all, those of us who have felt that a Rogerian approach is most valuable probably feel that way because we have compassion for others and unconditionally want to accept them. Why wouldn't any client bloom with such authentic caring, protection, and permission? If all my life I felt about others and wanted most to be unconditionally accepted myself, then surely others feel the same way.

Those of us who have believed that Dr. Ellis' approach is most valuable probably believe that way because we have strong opinions about what is important, and we want to help others clarify (decontaminate) their convictions. Why wouldn't any client benefit from having their irrational beliefs confronted, especially those that lead to emotional problems? And without the client needing to be accepted or loved? If all my life I had strong opinions, and wanted people to value my convictions, then surely others know how their emotions and behaviors are fashioned by their beliefs.

Those of us who have liked Gestalt Therapy, and how Dr. Perls does it, probably like it because we don't want anyone telling us what to think or believe—we want to experience "IT" ourselves. Let clients deal with the struggle. Trying "logic" doesn't really help. They've got to experience it themselves. Just sidestep, and let their top dog and under dog go for it. Then the client discovers how truly to be free and creatively alive. If all my life I wanted to be independent and free, and I found the secret, then surely others can experience that optimum satisfaction, fulfillment, and that growth is through taking personal responsibility.

My observation of Gloria was that she was at that time a Feeler–Feeler, in the process of phasing. If so, she would over adapt with a Please you Driver in First Degree Distress, show victim Drooper mask behavior in Second Degree Distress, play "Kick me" and "Stupid" while exhibiting cover-up feelings of hurt, sad, and confused, and she would have anger as her Phase issue.

Given those dynamics, a PTM trained therapist would connect with Emotions and a Comforting Channel and help Gloria feel her authentic anger under the hurt, sad, and confusion cover-up feelings. Asking Channel with either Thoughts or Opinions would be avoided. In classic therapy models, this means connecting with Rogerian and utilizing another model that helps Gloria realize and express her underlying anger – for example, Gestalt. A therapist trained in PTM would avoid a Rational Emotive approach, as it does not match Gloria's Perception, her Channel, or her psychological needs. Ironically, a steady offering of those Perceptions of Opinions and Thoughts, delivered through the Asking Channel, would have invited her *into* distress.

First, let's look at the comments each therapist made of his impressions of how his session with Gloria went. Dr. Rogers said, "All in all I feel good about this interview."[2] (Notice his Feeler Perception). Dr. Perls quipped, "Quite successful and consistent with my therapeutic outlook."[3] In an interview by Dr. Rosenthal,[4] Dr. Ellis stated that he was below his own par and tried to get too much (information) into the 20 plus minutes, commenting that if he had focused on one or two things it would have been better.

Dr. Rogers is the first to interview Gloria. His perceptual language of Emotion and unconditionally accepting her with his Comforting Channel clearly established a Feeler rapport. Gloria declares, "Gee, I'd like you for my father." Rogers responds, "You look to me like a pretty nice daughter."[5] Whether or not Dr. Rogers dealt with the transference/counter transference issues is not known; however, the consensus among observers is that he did connect significantly with her. In fact, Gloria stated that if she were beginning therapy she would like to work with Dr. Rogers.

Dr. Perls is the next to interview Gloria.[6] He does not use the Comforting Channel, but rather confronts her incongruity: "I'm aware of your smile, you don't believe a word of it. It's phony." He has apparently diagnosed her need to be aware of and express her anger. She even states, "I'd like to get mad at you." Perls pushes her further to be in touch with her anger: "I, I, I ,I…"

Dr. Perls: "How are you feeling right now?"

Gloria: "I don't know."

Dr. Perls: "You're playing stupid."

Gloria bemoans that she is feeling dumb and stupid, while kicking her feet. Dr. Perls again points out the incongruity of what she says and what she is doing: "What are you doing with your feet now?"

A PTM interpretation of Perls' therapy direction is consistent with helping a phasing Feeler to feel and express her anger authentically. Even after the interview Perls continued his message. As Dr. Rosenthal[7] records, "I shall use Gloria's verbatim account: 'After a full day of filming, the weariness was apparent in all of us. The doctors, the secretary, the producer, cameraman and I were standing in the foyer saying our good-byes, thank yous, etc. Dr. Perls was standing beside me smoking a cigarette, chatting with Dr. Ellis, when I suddenly noticed Dr. Perls was scanning the room with his eyes. He then made a motion to me with his hands as if to say, Hold Out your hand in cup-like form – palm up. Unconsciously I followed his request – not really knowing what he meant. He flicked his cigarette ashes in my hand. Insignificant? Could be – if one wouldn't mind being mistaken for an ashtray. Hmmm – do ashtrays kick their feet?'"

Although unsolicited, Perls' intervention again pointed out Gloria's victim position and invited her to become aware of her anger. She must have intuited the value of Perls' confrontations because among the three therapists, she chose Perls: "In this stage of the game, where am I right now, Dr. Perls could be the most valuable to me. So he isn't quite as coddling, but I think I could really get a lot from him although I'd want to battle with him too . . ."[8]

I concluded that Gloria was phasing – needing to feel her authentic Feeler anger – by the comment, "where am I right now, Dr. Perls could be the most valuable to me." Had she not been phasing, but rather wanted to deal with a non-phasing "problem" in her life, a therapist who offered Emotion, the Comforting Channel, and gave her recognition of person would have been ideal. As she herself admitted, if she were beginning therapy (*i.e.*, not Phasing) she would have liked to work with Dr. Rogers.

Gloria's experience with the Ellis session was that she couldn't keep up with him. This certainly makes sense in that Dr. Ellis' favorite Channel would have been Asking with Opinions and Thoughts as Perceptions. And since as a phasing Feeler she would have needed to feel her anger, Ellis'

REBT model would not have addressed her feeling angry, only at best the resulting value of it.

It is clear that the Rogerian approach worked best to establish a connection and that the Gestalt approach worked best to deal with the issue. A PTM therapist would have "combined" the two with Gloria, the Feeler-Feeler, by using the Comforter Channel and Emotions, and by encouraging authentic anger. A caution about using Gestalt in such a way as to identify or confront behavior is that it does not match the Perception of a Feeler. For the Phase anger issue work, I would have recommended the Goulding's Redecision Therapy approach. [9]

Chapter Notes:

[1] Shostrom, E.L. (Producer)."Three Approaches to Psychotherapy I, II, and III" [Film]. Psychological Films, 1965.

[2] Rosenthal, Howard. "Lessons from the Legend of Gloria - Were we duped by the world's most influential counseling session," *Counselor Magazine*, December 2005.

[3] *Ibid.*

[4] Rosenthal, Howard. "The REBT story you haven't heard: a no holds barred interview with Dr. Albert Ellis." *Journal of Clinical Activities, Assignments & Handouts in Psychotherapy Practice*, Vol. 2(3), 2002.

[5] *Ibid* at 2.

[6] *Ibid.*

[7] *Ibid.*

[8] *Ibid.*

[9] Goulding, Robert and Mary. "Injunctions, Decisions, and Redecisions," *TA Journal,* 1976.

Unit Fifteen
Using the Process Therapy
Model Profile Report

The PTMP identifies the positive, healthy personality structure of the client, what she will likely do in distress and why she does it. Only when/if the distress is intense and enduring enough will an Adaptation (clinical) designation be appropriate for that distressed behavior.

Chapter 1. Therapist's Personality Structure

It should be obvious that the personality structure of the therapist will determine her natural choice of Channel, Perception, and therapy model bias.

In the Process Communication Model® (PCM), the non-clinical management methodology based on PTM research and techniques, and the Process Education Model™ (PEM), its education-oriented variant, we have several research studies that show just how important the process is in interacting. Summaries of several of these studies are provided in Appendix E.

So, the therapist who knows his own personality structure will be aware of his natural tendencies to use favorite Channel(s) and Perception(s). Monitoring second-by-second and following PTM tenets will provide a therapy plan individualized to each client, while still allowing appropriate techniques and models.

Chapter 2. Process: Base and Phase

The PTMP report will give the client's personality structure and the potential Ware Adaptation; for example, John Doe is a Believer (Base)–Doer (Phase). This means that Mr. Doe primarily views the world through Opinions and is motivated in life by Incidence. This personality structure in prolonged Phase distress corresponds to the Ware Adaptation of Antisocial. These floors, any stages, and the next floor beyond the Phase will be given, along with the scores for each.

Chapter 3. Connecting

Four Channels will be identified in the PTMP, in order of the client's preference and with scores for each: Directing, Asking, Comforting, and Playing. Scores of 40 or more indicate "open" Channels. A score of 20 or less indicates infrequent use. The Channel of the Base is always strongest and the one in which the therapist should use to connect with the client. Mr. Doe's scores are: Asking 100, Directing 84, Comforting 74, and Playing 44.

Strong Perceptions (scores $\geq$ 60) will be identified and printed in order of use by the client: Thoughts, Emotions, Opinions, Reactions (likes/dislikes), Actions, or Inactions (reflections).

Mr. Doe's scores are: Opinions 100, Actions 86, and Emotions 76. Connecting with the Base Perception is recommended.

Since Mr. Doe is a Believer–Doer, connecting is best done with Asking Channel with Opinions.

Any Driver response is an advertisement that the client is no longer willing/able to move to the floor from which the therapist is offering her Channel and Perception.

Chapter 4. Psychological Needs

The PTMP will identify the client's Phase and Base psychological needs. The following is an example for our hypothetical client, Mr Doe:

Psychological needs are the powerful desires that motivate us personally and professionally. Once our physical needs are met (air, water, food, shelter, etc.) our psychological needs become our primary motivators. The most important psychological needs to be satisfied are those of our Phase. These are primary and crucial.

The need for Incidence motivates Mr. Doe to want a lot of excitement in a short period of time. He may like challenges, risks, or competition. A rush or a thrill fills the bill.

Although these Phase psychological needs are vital to Mr. Doe's personal and professional well-being, it is important that he be aware of how to get his foundation needs met regularly.

This Base need for Recognition of Work motivates Mr. Doe to be goal and achievement oriented. He takes pride in most everything he does. If something is worth doing, it certainly is worth doing well. He is not likely to devote his time and energy to a project unless he believes in it and is proud to be involved in it.

The other Base need for Recognition of Conviction motivates Mr. Doe to have strong beliefs and opinions. It is important for him to lead a life consistent with these beliefs, values, and opinions. Whenever possible he is likely to want to exercise his influence, impacting upon the growth and direction of others. He will resonate with others who share his high standards of integrity, dependability and trust.

Involving himself in circumstances where others acknowledge him with respect and admiration is of particular gratification in meeting his Recognition of Conviction need."

Chapter 5. Phase Miniscript

When Phase psychological needs are not met positively, a person attempts to get the same needs met, but negatively. The PTMP also presents this Phase miniscript sequence. For example, given Mr. Doe's order of Personality Types and that he is in a Doer Phase:[1]

1st Degree: Expects others to be strong.
    Words: "You ... (when talking about self)."
    Defense Mechanism: Seduction.
    Position: I'm OK–You're OK if you're strong.

2nd Degree: Failure Mechanism: Manipulates.
    Warning Signals:
        Sets up arguments, creates negative drama.
        Ignores or breaks rules.
    Myth: "I can make you feel bad emotionally."
    Position: I'm OK–You're Not OK.
    Mask: Blamer.
    Role: Persecutor looking for a Victim.
    Cover-up feeling: Vindictive.
    Primary Injunction: "Don't be close."
    Secondary Injunctions (Phase): "Don't belong."

Secondary Injunctions (Base/Stages):
"Don't enjoy."
Games: LYHF, Rapo, Schlamazel.

3rd Degree: Experiences negative Incidence and drama.
Payoff: Depressed and abandoned.

Current Phase Script: Always

Potential Issue

Long-term, intense distress, evidenced by frequent Second Degree behaviors, indicates the possibility of bonding as an unfinished issue.

Probable Impasse

The early decision is likely to be, "Things and people can make you feel bad." Therefore you will have to be strong and abandon anyone who gets too close. And as long as I can abandon you, I can avoid bonding to you."

* * * * * * *

The PTMP report identifies whether the client's distress is related to Phase or Base. In this case, the report identified Phase.

The first consideration for the therapist will be to connect with the client. Mr. Doe is Believer Base, so Asking with Opinions is the process choice.

The next thing to determine is if the client is Phasing. There are several ways to approach this. The most obvious is to ascertain whether the client has been experiencing recurring and severe Second Degree Distress, with intense warning signals, all of which is designed to avoid a significant "bonding" relationship.

236

Evidence to support this would include that: 1) there is a "retesting" of the bonding issue with a potential important close relationship that could result in either abandonment or intimacy; 2) this Doer Phase issue has not been tested in this Phase yet; 3) the client seldom experiences third degree distress of the Phase; and 4) the client does not stop the distress behavior when provided ample positive Doer Phase Incidence.

If this client is Phasing, then the focus of his therapy is to resolve his bonding issue. Confront his abandoning of others and support establishing relationships with protection and permission, while still encouraging symptomatic relief with positive Incidence homework.

Remember, for the Phasing Doer, the continuum of bonding ranges from being vindictive to being intimate.

As discussed previously, a therapy group setting with other knowledgeable, "sophisticated" Doer Base/Phase clients is recommended. In the case of Mr. Doe, who is Believer Base, initial one-to-one interactions with the therapist is important to first establish a connection of trust, exchange of information, and agreed upon therapy goals and direction.

PTM identifies "Probable Impasse," and suggests an "early decision." These terms and phrases were used by Dr. Bob and Mary Goulding, who originated Redecision Therapy, a powerful and valuable model of psychotherapy.[*][2] Although I retain their terms, and agree with a client making an early decision connecting Drivers and Second Degree consequences, the Driver and the Second Degree dynamics

---

[*] Mary Goulding continues to write and has training tapes available. I highly recommend learning about Redecision Therapy.

(injunctions) were already present within the personality structure. In other words, all Thinker Base individuals will have a Be perfect Driver, and "Don't feel grief" as the primary potential injunction. There is no decision about having this Driver, but rather its connection "consequences" awareness in relation to the client's early environment.

For example, the probable early decision for the Thinker is, "If I don't do the thinking for you, then something bad will happen. Therefore, I will be perfect and not make any mistakes and, as long as I am critical of you not thinking clearly, I can avoid my grief." The "decision" is not in regard to taking on Be perfect behavior, but rather in becoming aware of that defensive behavior and its relation to fantasized Second Degree consequences, natural to the individual's personality dynamics.

A Thinker would not (within that Personality Type floor structure) "decide" to Please others, Try hard for others, Be strong for others, expect others to Be Perfect, or expect others to Be strong. Nor does a Thinker's early decision involve a Be perfect Driver with consequences of another Personality Type's dynamic; for example, there would not be the decision, "As long as I am perfect, I won't grow up (Funster)."

PTM's identification of a Probable Impasse emphasizes the *awareness* of the already innate personality dynamics, and the Driver – Second Degree connecting "consequences" that are common in defending against resolving the issue.

If the client is not Phasing, but still showing the behaviors of Doer Phase distress, then the focus of the treatment is to get needs met positively and to resolve any primary or secondary injunctions. In the case of Mr. Doe, the PTMP identifies that with his personality structure of Believer Base, directly followed by Doer Phase, his primary injunction is "Don't be close," his secondary injunction (Phase) is "Don't belong," and his secondary injunction (Base/Stages) is "Don't enjoy."

Our focus would be on helping such a non-Phasing client to get his Phase needs met positively, but the block to this is likely to be his unresolved, secondary injunctions.

Although an apparent inborn defense for each Personality Type, our existing injunctions are a result of our Base, personality structure, and Phase combinations, the potential of which is mediated by the quality of parenting and its perceived reinforcement or extinguishment. Distressed parents are likely to reinforce the natural Personality Type injunctions of the child.

"Don't belong" and Don't enjoy" would be fruitful injunctions to explore and resolve, as blocks to getting Incidence needs met positively. In perspective, the more time spent in Second and Third Degree Distress because of these injunctions, the more problematic the Always script will be in Mr. Doe's personal and professional life. The more cornered he will feel, the more justified he will be in cornering others. This will include manipulations, specifically involving redefining contracts or agreements as he deems to fit his purpose.

Games based on getting negative Incidence may well escalate: Let's You and Him Fight (pitting two people or groups against one another); RAPO (over flirting, and then accusing the other person of having a dirty mind); and Schlamazel (make a mistake, get kicked, and turn the tables and demand an apology).

239

It is not enough just to redecide that it's OK to belong and to enjoy for Mr. Doe. He will need to have daily ways of getting his Incidence needs met positively, as well as his Base Believer needs of Recognition of Work and Recognition of Conviction. He will also need to have positive reinforcements for his new decisions: a significant on-going group experience and on-going feelings of joy, related to someone or something.

In either case of a Phasing or non-Phasing Mr. Doe, evidence of closure for him will be the ability for a sustained intimate relationship, as long as current Phase needs are being met positively, the capacity for joy, an active membership in a group (family more than qualifies), no personal or professional Always script (cornered problems), and no Games.[*]

Although Dr. Ware's Personality Adaptations article had not been published until January 1983, he had been trained by Dr. Bob and Mary Goulding in the early 1970's, and had been doing Redecsion Therapy with each of the six Personality Adaptations since 1979.

Chapter Notes

[1] Kahler, Taibi. T.AS.P., Taibi Kahler Associates, Inc., 1977.

---

[*] If he Phased, then it would be the needs of his next floor. If he did not need to Phase, then getting his Promoter Phase, Incidence needs met positively would be necessary.

Unit Sixteen.
Earth calling ...

PTM has both predictive and postdictive value. It identifies the correlation of Phase to specific psychological needs. Additionally, when an individual does not get these Phase psychological needs met positively, he will attempt to get the very same needs met negatively, with or without awareness. The behavioral evidence of this is reflected in that Phase Distress Sequence, thus providing predictability.

Chapter 1. Predicting What the Astronauts Do

I am honored to have worked with Terry McGuire, who has stated about me:

> In 1978, when astronaut selection was resumed in preparation for NASA's shuttle program, Dr. Kahler was invited to participate with me as a consultant in a selection cycle. As I conversed with the individual applicants, Dr. Kahler sat quietly and listened, only rarely asking a pertinent question. Ten to fifteen minutes into each interview, he would make a few notes on a piece of paper and place it on the floor. When each interview was completed, we would share our findings. To my amazement, he had been able to extract and commit to paper at least an equal amount of meaningful data about the applicant's personality structure in a fraction of the time it had taken me. My response was, 'I must learn how he does that.' Thus began a long and very satisfying personal and professional relationship that continues to grow and be enriched with the passage of time.

> I have had the opportunity in my walk of life to have known a number of "professional giants" in the fields of behavioral

science and medicine. Individuals of well-deserved national or international reputation, including Nobel Prize winners. I have had some remarkable teachers, but I am the most grateful for what I have learned from my continued contact with Taibi Kahler.

Terence McGuire, M.D., 1994

> B.S., Biology and Chemistry
>
> M.S., Physiology
>
> M.D., Board eligible in Internal Medicine.
>
> Board qualified in Psychiatry.
>
> Associate Professor, University of Texas Health Science Center, Department of Psychiatry.
>
> Examiner, American Boards of Psychiatry and Neurology.
>
> Lead Psychiatrist for Manned Space Flight, NASA, (1959-1996).
>
> Special Award from the American Medical Association for contributions to space medicine.
>
> Upcoming Colonel USAF (NZ) (Ret.) – Special recognition for studies in the psychophysiology of life-threatening stress.

Terry used the Process Model with our profile reports from that time to 1996, when he retired. He also confirms the predictive value of PTM. In five out of six missions in which there were significant distress behaviors and related communication problems, he predicted accurately which astronauts would escalate, and what their distressed behaviors would be.[*] In the sixth mission, the returning astronaut

---

[*] The reader might ask, "Then why did he select these astronauts?" The answer is that Dr. McGuire's responsibility for selection was limited to U.S. candidates. Many flights were joint ventures with other countries whose astronauts were not selected with regard to personality dynamics.

admitted, "If I had to be up one more day, I would have lost it."

Russia, it seems, was one such country ignoring personality compatibility. Terry tells of two cosmonauts, who were scheduled to share a lengthy mission. One of the daily rituals was to take a sample of each other's blood. As personality dynamics unfolded, "shuttlebutt" has it that one became more opinionated (Believer?) and the other more blameless (Funster?). While taking a daily blood sample, the latter "accidentally" poked the needle into the bone of the other. Now that's getting under one's skin.

After a few days sepsis set in, and the mission had to be cancelled.

Chapter 2. Psychohistory

My father died in WWII. My mother was depressed thereafter for many years and never talked about his war years. After her death in 1998, I found his diary among her things. What a gift.

I now know what my father was like, not from what he said so much, but how he said it: his Base and Phase, how he perceived the world, what his character strengths were, his dynamics, his motivations, his Distress Sequences, his Base Phasing behaviors, and more.

With PTM and PCM, you can bring those from your past into your present, by analyzing what they wrote. If you have a video, you have all five behavioral cues with which to confirm.

Let's practice with Lincoln's Gettysburg Address. As with the best speeches, the first half connects and the second half convinces.

Although we are limited to one speech and only word cues, what does this speech indicate his Personality Type Base and Phase were?

Start with the first half of the speech in bold, and make a frequency count of his Perceptions. See Appendix C for an assessment.

Lincoln's Gettysburg Address

Fourscore and seven years ago, our fathers brought forth on this continent, a new nation, conceived in liberty and dedicated to the proposition that all men are created equal.

Now we are engaged in a great Civil War, testing whether that nation, or any nation so conceived and so dedicated, can long endure.

We are met on a great battlefield of that war. We have come to dedicate a portion of that field as a final resting place for those who here gave their lives that that nation might live. It is altogether fitting and proper that we should do this. But in a larger sense, we cannot dedicate, we cannot

consecrate, we cannot hallow this ground. The brave men, living and dead who struggled here have consecrated it far above our poor power to add or detract. The world will little note nor long remember what we say here, but it can never forget what they did here.

It is for us the living rather to be dedicated here to the unfinished work which they who fought here have thus far so nobly advanced. It is rather for us to be here dedicated to the great task remaining before us - that from these honored dead we take increased devotion to that cause for which they gave the last full measure of devotion – that we here highly resolve that these dead shall not have died in vain, – that this nation under God shall have a new birth of freedom, and that government of the people, by the people, for the people shall not perish from the earth.

Gettysburg, November 19, 1863
Abraham Lincoln

The second part of the speech is from Lincoln's Phase, projecting his Phase psychological motivations onto his audience.

What is his Phase?

If Lincoln had been in a *Feeler* Phase, he would have wanted each of us to have remembered in our heart all that we felt for our loved ones and for those who suffered, because we are all one family.

If he had been in a *Thinker* Phase, he would have given a logical, step-by-step plan for forging ahead as a nation, with each of us accepting responsibility for accomplishing objectives on time.

If he had been in a *Believer* Phase, he would have expressed his opinion that we should dedicate ourselves to a cause that honors all those who died for our freedom.

If he had been in a *Dreamer* Phase, he would have suggested that each of us, in our own way, in the privacy of home, reflect on all that has happened, and on what it all means.

If he had been in a *Funster* Phase, he would have made some clever quips, used dry humor, or told a satirical story about siblings fighting with one another.

If he had been in a *Doer* Phase, he would have been dramatic, hard hitting, action oriented and telling us what would and would not be tolerated.

It is quite obvious that Lincoln was in a Believer Phase: "It is for us the living rather to be dedicated here to the unfinished work ..." However, with only this one piece of evidence, we cannot be as confident of his Base.

The point of this exercise is *not* to prove Lincoln's personality structure, but to show the possibility of PTM/PCM in applications to psychohistory and personal insights into those no longer with us.

With our interpretation of Perceptions, our limited results suggest that Lincoln could have been Thinker-Believer, with Doer next, followed by Feeler. Imagine what we could do with studying his letters, manuscripts, notes, and the "content" data of his life.

What do we know about a person with that structure?

Thinker Base indicates:

Thoughts as the primary Perception
Responsible, logical, organized
Democratic style of management
Computer part strongest
Asking Channel most used
One-on-one interactional preference
Psychological needs: Recognition of Work and Time Structure

Second floor: Opinions

Dedicated, observant, conscientious
Democratic style of management
Computer part
Asking Channel
One-on-one
Psychological needs: Recognition of Work and Conviction

Third floor: Actions

Adaptable, charming, persuasive
Autocratic style of management
Director part
Directing Channel
Group-to-group

Fourth floor: Emotions

Compassionate, sensitive, warm
Benevolent style of management
Comforter part
Comforting Channel
Group

The following diagram illustrates Lincoln's Thinker/Thinker Miniscript Sequence:

Thinker Base/Thinker Phase Miniscript Sequence
Psychological needs: recognition of work and time structure

1st Degree: **Driver** :Expects self to Be perfect.   **Defense Mechanism:** Rationalization
2nd Degree: **Failure Mechanism:** Over Controls

Warning Signals: Frustrated with those who don't think
                Critical about time, money, and responsibility

Myth: "I can make you feel bad emotionally."   **Position:** I'm OK - You're Not OK.

Mask: Attacker   **Role:** Persecutor looking for a Victim

Racket Emotions: Frustrated, guilty   **Games:** NIGYSOB; Uproar

Primary Injunction: "Don't feel grief";
Secondary Injunctions: "Don't have fun;" "Don't be close," "Don't enjoy".

3rd Degree: Experiences negative recognition for work or ideas

Payoff: Depressed and worthless
Potential Current Issue: Long-term, intense distress, evidenced by frequent
2nd degree behaviors, indicates the possibility of loss as an unfinished issue. The
                 underlying authentic feeling to experience is "I am sad"

Probable Impasse: The early decision is likely to be, "If I don't do the thinking for
     you, then something bad will happen. Therefore, I will be perfect and not make any
     mistakes, and as long as I am critical of you not thinking clearly I can avoid my grief."

Until Process Script

Having Phased through Thinker, Lincoln would have had a significant loss for which he did not grieve sufficiently. After a period of time in Thinker distress, and grieving, he would have Phased. His new Believer Phase would have looked like this:

Thinker Base/Believer Phase Miniscript Sequence
Psychological needs: recognition of work and convictions

1st Degree: **Driver** :Expects others to Be perfect. **Defense Mechanism:** Projection
2nd Degree: **Failure Mechanism:** Pushes beliefs

Warning Signals: Frustrated with those who don't believe the same
Critical and suspicious

Myth: "I can make you feel bad emotionally."   **Position:** I'm OK - You're Not OK.

Mask: Attacker   **Role:** Persecutor looking for a Victim

Racket Emotions: Frustrated, guilty   **Games:** NIGYSOB; Uproar

Primary Injunction: "Don't feel grief";
Secondary Injunctions: "Don't have fun;" "Don't be close," "Don't enjoy".

3rd Degree: Experiences negative recognition for work or ideas

Payoff: Depressed and worthless
Potential Current Issue: Long-term, intense distress, evidenced by frequent
2nd degree behaviors, indicates the possibility of loss as an unfinished issue. The
underlying authentic feeling to experience is "I am sad"

Probable Impasse: The early decision is likely to be, "If I don't do the thinking for
you, then something bad will happen. Therefore, I will be perfect and not make any
mistakes, and as long as I am critical of you not thinking clearly I can avoid my grief."

(left margin, vertical: Until Process Script)

We can only imagine the struggle President Lincoln
would have had in a Believer Phase, with the issue of being
perfectly competent with new (national) responsibilities.

Unit Seventeen
Personality Types, Miniscripts,
and Adaptations

A person's personality structure consists of an ordering (condominium) of six Personality Types, all the behaviors of which are healthy. The three degrees of distress that the individual experiences and demonstrates is his miniscript. This miniscript behavior is called an Adaptation when given a diagnosis.

Chapter 1. The Use of "Adaptation"

Since a vast majority of the general population does not have distressed behavior to the extent that it warrants a clinical diagnosis (the behavior, not the person), most of what has been presented as each Personality Type's miniscript has not been given a designated diagnosis.

Dr. Ware and I are in the process of profiling with PTM a sufficient numbers of patients whose distressed behaviors have been given a classical diagnosis, to test for correlations of the 4,320 possible combinations of the six Personality Type Bases and Phases.[*]

I have elected further to incorporate Dr. Ware's terminology of Adaptation for several reasons: 1) to identify when the miniscript sequence is severe enough to warrant a diagnosis; 2) to translate into traditional language for those

---

[*] Not to ignore the additional factors of the amount of energy on each floor.

classically trained; 3) to help the therapist with individualized information about the client that the computer program can generate; and 4) because Dr. Ware's abridging of classical diagnostic categories into continua of just six categories is so understandable to beginning, as well as seasoned, therapists.

Chapter 2. The Process Therapy Model Profile

By using the PTMP to profile a client, the therapist receives a report that identifies the client's Perceptions and the Personality Type miniscript Distress Sequence. This provides the therapist with guidance on how to connect with the client, where to focus, which technique (therapy model) to use, and which Channels and Perceptions to avoid.

Furthermore, as a monitoring model, PTM also provides the therapist with a second-by-second "Driver-meter" to assist in determining whether she is communicating or miscommunicating relative to the client's frame of reference.

Reliability and validity scores and a miniscript Distress Sequence for Phase and Base are provided with the PTMP. The report identifies which of these can be evaluated to the extent of being the current potential Adaptation upon which to focus in therapy.

Chapter 3. Is the Client Phasing?

The three degrees of distressed behavior of a Personality Type is the miniscript. The computer generated PTMP report is individualized to which one of the 4,320 combinations of the six Personality Type Bases and Phases the client possesses. Thus, each PTMP report varies in individualized identifications of script injunctions, games, and scripts. This is very valuable information for the therapist in determining the focus of treatment.

In working with the client, a first PTM consideration is to determine whether he is Phasing. Recall that this can be assessed by finding out if ample psychological needs of the Personality Phase are being made available and *accepted*. If they are not, and if the client is spending extended and intense time in Second Degree basement behavior of the miniscript, then the likelihood of Phasing is high. Final confirmation comes from exploring the relationship of the increasing amount of expected cover-up feeling when the issue is tested.

For example, a Thinker Phasing client is the star bowler on his company team. It is their last game of the year, and for the league championship.

A major traffic jam prevents him from getting to the event, until it is over.

Even with a substitute, his team wins the League Championship, but here's how he experienced the situation, and how he behaved.

While in the traffic jam, he realized that he would not be on time in order to participate in the championship match. Instead of feeling sad about this loss, he became enraged. Hitting and honking his horn, he hollered obscenities at the other drivers. If a police car had not been a few cars over in another lane, he would've gotten out of his car and challenged one of those "stupid *#*!^'s" to a fight.

When he arrived and learned that his teammates had won the League Championship, he didn't feel good about it. Instead of remembering all of the games he had helped his team win, he only thought of "Those damn stupid people!" who had caused the traffic jam.

He didn't congratulate his teammates, and he didn't hear his teammates thanking him.

To a trained PTM therapist, his response to the traffic jam evidences clearly that the loss of this opportunity was connected with a major loss related to this issue.

If the client isn't Phasing, his presenting problem is likely to be a symptom of not getting psychological needs met positively or an unresolved injunction. The PTMP will identify these injunctions as well as the script.

Knowing the client's personality structure also will give the therapist information as to which Channels and Perceptions to use to connect and to invite the client out of Driver behavior.

Whether the client is Phasing or not, the PTMP Homework Plan for getting psychological needs met positively on a daily and a weekly basis can be very valuable.

The Phase (and sometimes the Base) of the PTMP report will identify the miniscript distress behavior, which in turn determines the therapy plan. Severity of the miniscript behavior determines whether a diagnosis of Adaptation is warranted, as well as a classical one.

Chapter 4: The Miniscript as an "Adaptation"

Since it is the intensity and severity of the miniscript that determines whether that sequence of three degrees of distress will have a clinical designation of Adaptation, it is not appropriate or relevant to call a Personality Type an Adaptation.

Personality Types refer to the six types that make up a person's personality structure [condominium], all of which are OK.

Therefore, we are not addressing an Adaptation when we select a Channel or Perception, but rather attempting to connect with a Personality Type.

However, if a client were in First Degree Distress (Driver) of an Adaptation, we could use a therapeutic intervention of selecting the appropriate Channel and Perception to invite her out of this Driver. Similarly, we could be addressing a Second Degree Adaptation mask by offering the appropriate and matching positive psychological need.

A Personality Type/Phase miniscript sequence can be considered Adaptation when that behavior impairs or significantly interferes with the capacity to meet the ordinary demands of life. Since an Adaptation refers to a diagnostic continuum ranging from base line clinical symptoms to severe ones, an Adaptation could include delusions and prominent hallucinations.

Whether the miniscript is an Adaptation or not, the issue is likely to be the same.

Miniscript	Issue	Potential Adaptation
Thinker	**Loss**	**Obsessive-Compulsive**
Feeler	**Anger**	**Hysterical**
Believer	**Fear**	**Paranoid**
Doer	**Bonding**	**Antisocial**
Dreamer	**Autonomy**	**Schizoid**
Funster	**Responsibility**	**Passive-Aggressive**[*]

However, connecting with each of these still depends on what the client's Base Personality Type is.

The Assessing Matrix®

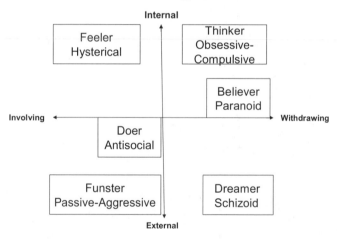

---

[*] Dr. Ware chooses to keep the Adaptation of Passive-Aggressive although the latest DSM does not recognize this as a Personality Disorder. I am in complete agreement with his decision, as it encompasses several other categories.

Thinker Miniscript: Obsessive-Compulsive Adaptation
Psychological needs: recognition of work and time structure

Until* Process Script

1st Degree: **Driver** :Expects self to Be perfect.   **Defense Mechanism:** Rationalization
Difficulty in delegating: I can do it better and faster

2nd Degree: **Failure Mechanism:** Over Controls

Warning Signals: Frustrated with those who don't think, don't follow the rules, or make mistakes. Issues about time, money, responsibility, order, cleanliness, details. Hoarding.

Myth: "I can make you feel bad emotionally."   **Position:** I'm OK - You're Not OK.

Mask: Attacker

Role: Persecutor looking for a Victim

Cover-up Emotions: Frustrated, guilty   **Games*:** NIGYYSOB, Uproar

Primary Injunction*: Don't feel grief
Secondary Injunctions*: Don't have fun, Don't be close, Don't enjoy.

3rd Degree: Experiences negative recognition for work or ideas

Payoff: Depressed and worthless
Potential Current Issue: Long-term, intense distress, evidenced by frequent 2nd degree behaviors, indicates the possibility of loss as an unfinished issue. The underlying authentic feeling to experience is "I am sad"

Probable Impasse: The early decision is likely to be, "If I don't do the thinking for you, then something bad will happen. Therefore, I will be perfect and not make any mistakes, and as long as I am critical of you not thinking clearly I can avoid my grief."
* computer generated

Feeler Miniscript: Hysterical Adaptation
Psychological needs: recognition of person and sensory

After* Process Script

1st Degree: **Driver** :Expects self to Please.   **Defense Mechanism:** Introjection
Over adapts to impress

2nd Degree: **Failure Mechanism:** Makes mistakes

Warning Signals: Invites criticism, shows self doubt, denigrates self, exaggerates emotion, self-dramatic

Myth: "You can make me feel bad emotionally." **Position:** I'm Not OK - You're OK.

Mask: Drooper

Role: Victim looking for a Persecutor

Cover-up Emotions: Sad, confused, hurt, unappreciated   **Games*:** Kick me, Stupid

Primary Injunction*: Don't feel angry
Secondary Injunctions*: Don't be important, Don't grow up

3rd Degree: Experiences unconditional rejection as a person

Payoff: Depressed and unloved
Potential Current Issue: Long-term, intense distress, evidenced by frequent 2nd degree behaviors, indicates the possibility of anger as an unfinished issue. The underlying authentic feeling to experience is "I am angry".

Probable Impasse: The early decision is likely to be, "If I express my anger at you I will have hurt your feelings and/or you will reject me. Therefore, I will please you and hold in my anger."
* Computer generated

256

Believer Miniscript: Paranoid Adaptation
Psychological needs: recognition of convictions and work.

Until* (professional) Process Script

1st Degree: Driver :Expects others to Be perfect. **Defense Mechanism:** Projection
Focuses on what's wrong, not what's right

2nd Degree: Failure Mechanism: Pushes beliefs

Warning Signals: Frustrated with those who do not believe the same.
Unforgiving, hypervigilant. Stereotypes others as distrustful, disloyal, hurtful.

Myth: "I can make you feel bad emotionally." **Position:** I'm OK - You're Not OK.

Mask: Attacker   **Role:** Persecutor looking for victim

Cover-up Emotions: Righteous, distrustful, **Games*:** NIGGYSOB, Why Don't You
suspicious, jealous

Primary Injunction*: Don't trust
Secondary Injunctions*: Don't be close. Don't enjoy. Don't belong.

3rd Degree: Experiences negative recognition of convictions

Payoff: Depressed and hopeless

Potential Current Issue: Long-term, intense distress, evidenced by frequent
2nd degree behaviors, indicates the possibility of fear as an unfinished issue.
The underlying authentic feeling to experience is "I am afraid".

Probable Impasse: The early decision is likely to be, "If I don't make sure you believe
the right way and do the right things, then something bad will happen. Therefore I
expect you to be perfect and not make any mistakes; and as long as I am preaching
at you, I can avoid my own fears."

* Computer generated

Doer Miniscript: Antisocial Adaptation
Psychological need: incidence

Always* Process Script

1st Degree: Driver :Expects others to Be strong. **Defense Mechanism:** Seduction
Fend for yourself

2nd Degree: Failure Mechanism: Manipulates

Warning Signals: Sets up arguments. Creates negative drama. Does illegal things.
Contentious. Bellicose. Irresponsible. Deceitful. Impulsive. Disregard for (safety of) others

Myth: "I can make you feel bad emotionally." **Position:** I'm OK - You're Not OK.

Mask: Blamer   **Role:** Persecutor looking for victim

Cover-up Emotions: Vindictive, remorseless **Games*:** LYHF, RAPO, Schlimazel

Primary Injunction*: Don't be close. .
Secondary Injunctions*: Don't trust. Don't make it. Don't belong

3rd Degree: Experiences negative incidence and drama

Payoff: Depressed and abandoned

Potential Current Issue: Long-term, intense distress, evidenced by frequent
2nd degree behaviors, indicates the possibility of bonding as an unfinished issue.
The underlying authentic feeling to experience is "I feel intimate".

Probable Impasse: The early decision is likely to be, "Things and people can make
you feel bad. Therefore you will have to be strong and abandon anyone who gets too
close. And as long as I abandon you, I can avoid intimacy and bonding with you."

* Computer generated

Dreamer Miniscript: Schizoid Adaptation
Psychological need: Solitude

1st Degree: Driver :Expects self to Be strong.   **Defense Mechanism:** Dissociation
                 Detached

2nd Degree: **Failure Mechanism:** Withdraws

     Warning Signals: Passively waits. Projects started and not finished. Avoids physical and emotional closeness. Few friends. Indifferent to praise or criticism. Detached.

       Myth: "You can make me feel bad emotionally." **Position:** I'm Not OK - You're OK.

       Mask: Drooper   **Role:** Victim looking for persecutor

       Cover-up Emotions: Insignificant. Inadequate.   **Games:**

       Primary Injunction*: Don't make it
       Secondary Injunctions*: Don't belong. Don't have fun. Don't be close.
                       Don't be important.

3rd Degree: Experiences negative solitude

       Payoff: Depressed and listless

       Potential Current Issue: Long-term, intense distress, evidenced by frequent 2nd degree behaviors, indicates the possibility of autonomy as an unfinished issue.
           The underlying authentic experience is "I feel potent".

       Probable Impasse: The early decision is likely to be, "Things and people can make me feel bad. Therefore I will be strong and withdraw, and as I become passive, I can avoid making my own decisions."

         * Computer generated

Funster Miniscript: Passive-Aggressive Adaptation
Psychological need: Contact (playful)

1st Degree: Driver :Expects self to Try Hard.   **Defense Mechanism:** Displacement
                 Sets up others to do for

2nd Degree: **Failure Mechanism:** Blames

     Warning Signals: Negative and complaining. Blameless and blameful. Stubborn. Hostile. .Procrastinative (forgetful). Impatient. Avoidant of responsibility. Deliberately inefficient.

       Myth: "You made me feel bad, so I'll make   **Position:** I'm OK - You're Not OK.
               make you feel worse."   **Role:** Persecutor looking for a Victim

       Mask: Blamer

       Cover-up feelings: Vengeful, bored   **Games*:** Yes but; SWYMMD; IWFY;
                                           Corner; Schlemiel
       Primary Injunction*: Don't grow up
       Secondary Injunctions* : Don't make it. Don't be close

3rd Degree: Experiences negative contact

       Payoff: Depressed and helpless

       Potential Current Issue: Long-term, intense distress, evidenced by frequent 2nd degree behaviors, indicates the possibility of responsibility as an unfinished issue.
           The underlying authentic feeling to experience is "I am sorry".

       Probable Impasse: The early decision is likely to be, "If you don't do the thinking for me, then I won't be happy. Therefore, I will be Try hard. When you don't make me feel good by thinking for me, then it is your fault. I feel bad, and as long as I blame you I can avoid taking responsibility for making myself feel good with self love."

         * Computer generated

Postscript:
Training in PTM and
Treating Adaptations

Licensed therapists who wish to purchase the Process Therapy Model Profile may do so by contacting us at Taibi Kahler Associates and providing proof of licensure.

Therapists should be aware that there are several persons and groups both within and outside the United States who purport to be proficient in teaching the concepts contained in this book. Unless the person's name, or that of the organization with which he or she is associated, is posted on our website or is so identified by one of our international affiliates (who also are identified on our website), they have not been certified to train PTM, their skills have not been evaluated by us, and they do not have access to the PPI or any of its outputs, including the PTMP.

We strongly recommend that therapists complete a course in PTM before engaging in its use. Practicing the techniques in a controlled environment while being observed by trained experts is critical for their effective use. Participants practice connecting using Perceptual language and Channels, energizing Personality Parts, recognizing Drivers and Second Degree Distress, intervention techniques, as well as other skills.

PTM Seminars are available for clinicians who wish to learn about how to use PTM, as well as those who would like to become certified to teach these seminars. Please contact us by email at kahlercom@aristotle.net or go to www.processtherapymodel.com for more information.

Dr. Paul Ware has created a series of seminars to teach therapists how to interview for a classical diagnosis, confirm the Adaptation, and outline a course of treatment including appropriate medications and techniques. These seminars provide a solid foundation for learning how to do therapy with each Adaptation, including proven techniques of Redecision Therapy. Please contact us at kahlercom@aristotle.net for current information on Dr. Ware's seminars.

Appendix A-1

Ian Stewart BA Oxon PhD
Teaching and Supervising Transactional Analyst, ITAA/EATA
Registered Psychotherapist, UK Council for Psychotherapy
Master Practitioner, Society of Neuro-Linguistic Programming
New Barn, Wycomb, Melton Mowbray, Leicestershire LE14 4QG, England
Telephone and Fax: (0)1664-444652; email: ian@theberne.com

23 September 2005

Dr Taibi Kahler,
Taibi Kahler Associates,
11815 Hinson Road,
Little Rock, AR 72212,
USA.

Dear Taibi,

Thank you for your letter of 28 June 2005 and for the enclosures you sent with it.

I have carefully read through all the materials you sent, with particular attention to the four requests you put to Vann and myself in the fifth paragraph of your letter.

I also faxed the materials through to Vann, and he and I have noted the points you raised. Vann, like me, is more than happy to comply with the four requests you put to us regarding assurances as to how we present your material, and so I am now replying to you on Vann's behalf as well as my own.

We now therefore formally give you the following assurances:

(1) Neither of us is claiming, will ever claim or would wish to claim, the originality of the material you have integrated. If anything we have written gives or seems to give the impression that we are so claiming, this was unintentional on our part, and we apologise to you for it.

(2) Neither of us is calling what we ourselves do, the "Process Model", nor will we ever use that designation for what we do.

(3) We acknowledge that what we call the Process Model in our book and teachings, integrating types [adaptations] with Drivers, channels [modes], process scripts, Assessing Matrix, and other dynamics that you have integrated and presented and copyrighted, is your Process [Therapy] Model.

(4) In any future editions and presentations we will update and credit what you have done accurately and with your prior approval.

As well as giving these formal assurances, we want to add: we see your Process Therapy Model as a major advance in the field of psychotherapy and human understanding. We greatly admire the creativity, clear thinking and close observation on your part that allowed you to develop your Process Therapy Model. We have always seen ourselves, as writers and

261

TA trainers, simply as "messengers" carrying your message to the psychotherapy and counselling trainees to whom we present. Though we have carried this message, the message itself has always been yours, not ours, and we have done our best at all times to make this clear.

What we have learned from your recent communications is that we have not succeeded in making it clear enough that we were only messengers. Further, that the message we have been carrying has been one that was out of date. We are sorry about both these things, and we assure you that before embarking on any future writings on this subject matter, we will contact you in the way you suggest, invite you to give us the updated information you have developed, and negotiate with you for the rights to that information. In verbal presentations, we shall ensure to the best of our ability that we incorporate the updated theory and applications that you have included in the materials you have sent us.

We thank you for confronting us in such a clear and OK manner, and we hope that our response is equally clear and is in line with your wishes.

We look forward to being in touch with you and to learning further from you in future.

With all good wishes,

Ian Stewart and Vann Joines

Appendix A-2

Dr. Michael Brown & Associates
15272 Yorkshire Lane, Huntington Beach, CA 92467
Phone: (714) 893-2673 Fax: (714) 908-7614 Email: michael@drmichaelbrown.com

June 29, 2005

To: Dr. Taibi Kahler
Taibi Kahler Associates
11815 Hinson Rd.
Little Rock, AR 72212

Dear Taibi:

I am writing in reference to information written in two books I co-authored with Stan Woollams: *Transactional Analysis: A Modern and Comprehensive Text of TA Theory and Practice* (Huron Valley Institute Press, 1976) and *TA: The Total Transactional Analysis Handbook (Prentice-Hall, 1977)*.

In those books, with your permission, Dr. Woollams and I presented a section dedicated to Script Process and Intervention, including various ways of confronting each of the Script Process types. This information was based directly on your research, including your validated questionnaire for therapists to use with clients on scripts, Drivers, rackets, games, phases, injunctions, impasses, etc., and in-depth understanding of how to confront scripts. Our primary sources for that information were your writings as well as a series of lectures that you presented on Script Process and Intervention at Huron Valley Institute and other locations. We also verified this information with you personally before submitting the books for publication.

Although the information presented was accurate and up-to-date at that time of publication, we are also aware that you continued to refine, develop and add to these ideas over the years as you integrated them into a much larger theory known as Process Therapy Model. I have personally observed the evolution of your research and ideas into what I consider to be one of the pre-eminent theories in the field of modern Psychology, and we are very proud to have been among the first to recognize your important contributions in our early works.

Sincerely,
Dr. Michael Brown

Appendix B

The following is an October 7, 2007 email from Dr. Sue Geier, retired Director of the Brevard Community College Lab Schools to Dr. Taibi Kahler:

Hey, Taibi.

The number of children observed can vary widely – depending upon how narrow or broad we define the criteria. I figure apprx. 30,000 is a conservative figure.

I listed named, number of years in Lab School times number of children in classes. Here, I know we used your information in order to help explain temperament and behavior to parents. Those who were not in Lab School, I broadly estimated numbers.

Example:

Janet Helfand	20 (3-5 yr. olds)	x 1 class	x 4 years =	80
Joan Ruppert	20 (1-2 yr. olds)	x 2 classes	x 8 years =	320
Tanya Walker	30 (1-5 yr. olds)	x 1 class	x 5 years =	150
Wendy Potter	20 (3-5 yr. olds)	x 1 class	x 16 years =	320
Barbara Young	40 (1-5 yr. olds)	x 16 classes	x 16 years =	3200
Sue Geier	40 (1-5 yr. olds)	x 16 classes	x 16 years =	5000
Others				
Mary Ernst	Mostly			2000 teens
Ernie Flanagin	Mostly			2000 teens
Russell Vann – rs.	All ages	30/day	5000/yr x 27 rs.	13000
Total				26070

If you add in people I have forgotten – like Gail Buchanan – I think 30000 is conservative.

Congratulations on writing the book! We – the world – certainly could benefit from the information.

264

Appendix C

Lincoln's Gettysburg Address

<u>Fourscore and seven years ago,</u> <u>our fathers</u> **brought forth** <u>on this continent,</u> <u>a new nation,</u> <u>conceived in liberty</u> and *dedicated* <u>to the proposition</u> <u>that all men</u> **are created** *equal.*

<u>Now</u> <u>we</u> **are engaged** <u>in a</u> *great* <u>Civil War,</u> <u>testing whether that nation,</u> <u>or any nation</u> <u>so conceived</u> *and so dedicated,* **can** <u>long</u> **endure.**

<u>We</u> **are met** <u>on a</u> *great* <u>battlefield</u> <u>of that war.</u> <u>We</u> **have come** *to dedicate* <u>a portion</u> <u>of that field</u> <u>as a final</u> <u>resting place</u> <u>for those</u> <u>who</u> <u>here</u> **gave** *their lives* <u>that</u> <u>that nation</u> *might live.* <u>It is altogether</u> *fitting* and *proper* <u>that we</u> *should do* <u>this.</u> <u>But in a larger sense,</u> <u>we cannot</u> *dedicate,* <u>we cannot</u> *consecrate,* <u>we cannot</u> *hallow* <u>this ground.</u> <u>The brave men,</u> <u>living and dead</u> <u>who</u> **struggled** <u>here</u> *have consecrated* <u>it</u> <u>far above</u> <u>our poor power</u> <u>to add or detract.</u> <u>The world will little note</u> <u>nor long remember</u> <u>what we say</u> <u>here,</u> <u>but it can never forget</u> <u>what they</u> **did** <u>here.</u>

Perceptions: Although we have only words, here's one interpretation:

2 Feeler Emotions in *<u>Italics and underlined</u>.*

9 Doer Actions are in **bold.**

13 Believer Opinions are in *Italics*

51 Thinker Thoughts are <u>underlined</u>.

Appendix D
Validation Studies

The Personality Pattern Inventory (PPI) has its foundations in behavioral psychology and was originally designed to identify positive and negative characteristics of individuals (1972).

Of major importance to this Process Communication Model® (PCM) is the research findings (1982) that a person is motivated by certain psychological needs, and that if these needs are not met positively, then the person will attempt to get the exact same psychological (motivational) needs met *negatively*, through very predictable non-productive behaviors in his/her personal and professional life, *with* or *without* awareness.

These basic psychological needs are tied to (correlated with) phases of a person's life and determine the individual's positive and negative motivations.

The PPI can predict normal and severe distress sequences for the individual.

Further research yielded correlations with standard management and communication concepts.

Again, since this is a model based in personality theory and psychological dynamics, the results allow cross-cultural utilization. The Personality Pattern Inventory has been administered to more than 700,000 men and women in the United States (October 2007); it has been translated into Spanish, German, French, Flemish, Finnish, Korean, Romanian, Norwegian, Danish, Italian, and Japanese, and it has been taught on 5 continents.

The PPI was used by Dr. Terry McGuire of NASA from 1992 – 1996 in the selection of astronauts and payload specialists because of its accuracy in predicting individual distress sequences, as well as assessing compatibility.

As of January 1, 2008, nine dissertations have been completed on the model with doctorates awarded.

As the Personality Pattern Inventory (PPI) was first conceived, the following five elements germane to the experimental design construction were considered:

1. That a set of questions is administered to each participant in a structured manner to ensure that the method of administration remains consistent across different persons giving and taking the inventory.
2. That the responses to the inventory are considered to be a sample of his or her behavior.
3. That a number is assigned to each response that inferences can be drawn about the participant's possession of the variable or traits measured by the inventory.
4. That objective measures must be taken in the assigning of numerals and in inferring the quantity of the trait possessed.
5. That reliability and validity measures must be determined by objective, empirical procedures.

Two key words in understanding the essence of good empirical design are reliability and validity. Reliability means accuracy. Procedures for determining reliability are procedures for measuring the accuracy of a test. In other words, the degree to which a participant's inventory score reflects his Personality Type, rather than the effects of error.

Validity addresses the question, "Does the inventory yield the information that it was designed to?"

Face, concurrent, and predictive validity are all relevant to the PPI. Face validity refers to the participant's impression that the PPI measures what he or she thinks, feels, or believes that it did. Concurrent validity refers to the focus of the inventory to produce an assessment of the participant into one of the six Personality Types. Predictive validity refers to the predicting of the participant whether or not he or she will develop a criterion-state, such as a given Failure Pattern or new, open Channel of Communication.

The following steps and procedures were carried out in the development of the PPI:

In psychology and psychiatry, clinical diagnostic categories are used to identify clusters of maladaptive behavior patterns in order to understand the underlying dynamics and to determine a treatment plan.

Trained "experts," usually psychologists and psychiatrists, are called on to use their clinical skills of observation and evaluation to diagnose a person, *i.e.*, give a name to the maladaptive behavior pattern that has been officially defined and described in the diagnostic and Statistical Manual III. Such widely used tests as the Minnesota Multiphasic Personality Inventory are often administered to determine diagnoses.

In 1972, the Kahler Transactional Analysis Script Checklist was taken by 990 people. Ten items were ranked (Drivers) nine items were open-end responses, and seventy-eight items were judged agree or disagree. These Drivers were: 1. be perfect 2. please 3. be strong 4. try hard 5. hurry up

Each of these was positioned to be aimed at self or others. They also were presented as conditional. For example, the be perfect forms were: "I am OK if I am perfect" and "You are OK if you are perfect." Correlating these ten item Drivers with the seventy-eight personality variables yielded few high correlations, except with those items that identified the themes of scripts. (>.25) This did, however, provide the author with insight into discovering the reinforcement pattern of sentence structures and counterscripts (Drivers) in the formulation of the life script.

The following high, but not significant, correlations were discovered between the Driver "types" and life script themes:

"Type"	Life Script
I'll please you	After
I'll be perfect for you	Until
You be perfect for me	Until
I'll be strong for you	Never
I'll try hard for you	Always
You be strong for me	Always
I'll try hard to please you and please you	Over & Over (Almost I)
I'll be perfect for you or you be perfect for me and I'll please you	Open End (Almost II)

With completed responses by 982 of the 990 who took the TASP (originally handed out to 1200), six of the ten Drivers were selected as the most experienced. The four that were never identified as being experienced first and most often were: 1) you please me, 2) you try hard for me, 3) I'll hurry up for you, and 4) you hurry up for me.

The following demographics were available:

N=(982)		
Type	Females (524)	Males (458)
I'll please you (363) 37%	298 O:3, B:13, W:282	65 B:1, W:54
I'll be perfect for me (206) 21%	41 B: 5, W: 36	165 O:7, B:12, W:14
You be perfect for me (137) 14%	22 B:2, W:20	115 B:8, W:107
I'll be strong for you (78) 8%	42 W:42	36 B:1, W:35
I'll try hard for you (167) 17%	112 B:12, W:100	55 B:9, W:46

You be strong for me (31) 3%	9 B:1, W:8	22 B:8, W:14

Later in the middle seventies this author considered personality types not just as maladaptive behaviors but also to include the complementary positive behaviors as well.

Six Personality Types were identified based on the general personality clusters associated with six of the Drivers in the original study: Reactor (please you), Workaholic (be perfect for you), Persister (be perfect for me), Dreamer (be strong for you), Rebel (try hard for you), and Promoter (be strong for me). With Kahler's (1978) theory of Process Therapy, positive patterns of behavior were associated with each Personality Type, yielding both positive and negative (maladaptive) behavior patterns.

In 1982, three "experts" in assessing the six Personality Types independently interviewed 100 people. All six Personality Types were represented in the sample. All three judges agreed on 97 assessments: A and B on 98, A and C on 97, and B and C on 99, thus yielding high inter-judge reliability (significant as >.001).

These same experts were also asked to determine "phase," or the current mode of Personality Type behavior. Using again Kendall's coefficient of concordance, W, and testing this significance with the critical values of chi-square, inter-judge reliability was again significant as >.001.

An additional number of people were assessed and selected by the judges independently so that a minimum number of 30 persons were available for each classification of Personality Type, yielding a total sample of 180 identified "assessed" people.

Two hundred and thirteen items including extractions from the original study item pool were administered to 112 randomly selected subjects. Analysis of this data indicated a "natural" loading on six criteria – the six Personality Types.

Two hundred and four of these items were administered to the 180 identified Personality Types. Only items with a correlation of greater than .60 (significant at >.01) were accepted for inclusion in the final Personality Pattern Inventory.

Two forms of the PPI were constructed from these significant items. Both forms have twenty-two items, with six answers each to be ranked by the participant. This yields a score on each of the Personality Type scales. The following correlations are reported for items and scales for each form:

KENDALL CORRELATIONS

Original Items	PCM 1 2	Reactors	Workaholics	Promoters	Rebels	Persisters	Dreamers	X
1.	X	.89	.77	.44	.77	.54	.72	.69
2.	X	.96	.94	.62	.79	.65	.85	.80
3.	X X	.67	.95	.83	.88	.77	.64	.79
4.	X	.93	.85	.59	.56	.42	.72	.68
5.	X X	.95	.80	.70	.78	.76	.76	.79
6.	X	.67	.88	.64	.56	.54	.76	.68
7.	X X	.94	.95	.87	.82	.55	.72	.81
8.	X	.82	.91	.70	.72	.67	.75	.76
9.	X	.64	.92	.54	.62	.60	.73	.68
10.	X	.97	.94	.76	.83	.62	.52	.77
11.	X X	.79	.75	.81	.75	.61	.72	.74
12.	X	.66	.77	.83	.62	.58	.76	.70
13.	X	.95	.92	.82	.62	.50	.86	.78
14.	X X	.99	.78	.74	.72	.75	.71	.78
15.	X	.93	.68	.62	.65	.73	.90	.75
16.	X X	.99	.84	.48	.83	.51	.66	.72
17.	X X	.90	.71	.75	.71	.6	.90	.77
18.	X	.64	.94	.53	.71	.91	.65	.73
19.	X X	.95	.91	.85	.74	.51	.63	.77
20.	X	.96	.71	.64	.70	.64	.88	.76
21.	X	.79	.94	.50	.75	.51	.74	.71
22.	X X	.96	.68	.77	.72	.66	.57	.73
23.	X X	.54	.73	.88	.60	.70	.66	.69
24.	X	.74	.84	.62	.62	.40	.71	.66
25.	X	.60	.89	.57	.45	.66	.64	.64
26.	X	.64	.58	.72	.64	.56	.58	.62
27.	X	.78	.57	.75	.72	.70	.70	.70
28.	X	.66	.94	.70	.50	.62	.57	.67
29.	X	..60	.66	.85	.65	.62	.57	.66
30.		.42	.70	.77	.54	.75	.87	.68
31.	X	.64	.77	.72	.74	.75	.77	.73
32.	X X	.94	.85	.635	.70	.62	.58	.67
33.	X	.70	.64	.55	.57	.79	.40	.61
34.	X	.56	.73	.81	.47	.77	.76	.66

271

Personality	Type	Reactors	Workaholics	Promoters	Rebels	Persisters	Dreamers
PCM$_1$	X's:	.80	.79	.71	.69	.64	.70
PCM$_2$	X's:	.82	.83	.72	.69	.63	.70
PPI (1&2)	X's:	.81	.81	.72	.69	.63	.70
PCM$_1$	X=.72						
PCM$_2$	X=.73						
PPI (1&2)	X=.73	Significant at .0001 level					

The original study did not demonstrate significant correlations between the six major groupings of Driver (types) and those expected item responses (comprised mainly of descriptions of negative, distressed behaviors).

The author viewed these six Driver types analogous to personality condominiums.

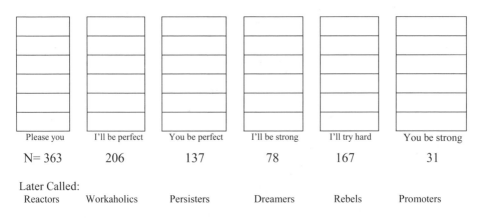

Please you	I'll be perfect	You be perfect	I'll be strong	I'll try hard	You be strong
N= 363	206	137	78	167	31

Later Called:

| Reactors | Workaholics | Persisters | Dreamers | Rebels | Promoters |

With the theory of phase, or a time in some people's lives where they experience being another Personality Type, especially demonstrating negative behaviors when in distress, a revisiting of the original data was warranted.

This time, no matter what type – Reactor, Workaholic, Persister, Dreamer, Rebel, or Promoter – expected item responses of the Driver phase (negative behaviors) were analyzed.

Review of evidence gathered in earlier studies demonstrated that the original theory needed refinement. A new hypothesis, to be tested, was called for. Two distinct procedures were developed and performed: 1) specify a "refined" hypothesis subsequent to review and analysis of prior results; and 2) design a protocol such that the "refined" hypothesis would be well and correctly tested.

Refining theory and hypothesis began with the identification of six (6) Personality Types and the confirmation of the primary Driver for each type. Secondly, "Phases" were postulated (Phase distress). These behaviors were related (associated) to a given Personality Type, as defined by the Driver phase the person was experiencing in his foreground – not necessarily the Driver Personality Type, as originally hypothesized. The original research did not include the critical importance of this phase concept. Hence the "refined" hypothesis was crafted to include the concepts of "Base" and "Phase."

Next a design of a statistical testing protocol was undertaken. Returning to previously gathered data, all checklists that had ranked one of the following Drivers as primary were included in the sample: I'll be perfect for you; You be perfect for me; I'll be strong for you; You be strong for me; I'll please you; and, I'll try hard for you. This resulted in a population of 982 cases. These cases were composed of undergraduates, graduate students, faculty members, friends, associates, and clients residing in West Lafayette, Indiana. (Note: there were *no* active psychotics included.) Since the (1982) study indicated significant (at the o.001 level) correlations between Driver and Personality Types *and* Phases, a reclassification of the original data was possible. This reclassification allowed testing of correlations between Driver phase and the seventy-eight personality variables. This "test" examined the correlation of *Phase* Driver with each "agree" or "disagree" response. This was adequate as the (1982) study confirmed that phase Personality Type negative personality variables are those observable under (normal) distress.

The results of the above protocol supported the design of the PPI to include both Base and Phase metrics. (Note: only traits that were significant at greater than the 0.05 level were included.)

Each form of PPI is designed to overcome a participant from endorsing socially desirable items (fake good) and from endorsing socially unusual or uncommon responses (fake bad).

By examining the responses relative to the normal characteristics of each Personality Type scale, a "questionable validity" comment may be assigned, as well as levels of confidence for both base and phase. Interview techniques by experts in Process Communication could also determine this.

Relative Manager Scores and Relative Interaction Scores for all six Personality Types are recorded and statistical procedures are performed to help determine usefulness.

Also available are confidence levels for both phase and base, as well as a validity statement.

For both model and management printouts the following distribution statistics apply:

Phase Confidence Levels

X (mean) = 52
S.D. (standard deviation) = 14

Standard Deviation	-2	-1	0	+1	+2
Score	24	38	52	66	80
Percentile Ranking	2	16	50	84	98

Base Confidence Levels

X (mean) = 74
S.D. (standard deviation) = 24

Standard Deviation	-2	-1	0	+1	+2
Score	26	50	74	98	
Percentile Ranking	2	16	50	84	

The higher the score, the greater the degree of confidence that the phase and base is accurate. A very low score is most often a sign of questionable validity.

Questionable Validity is identified when the information given on the inventory is analyzed and the results do not fall within statistical limits to insure that the profile is a clear and accurate picture of the person.

Also printed when there is Questionable Validity will be FGC (Fake Good Conscious), FGU (Fake Good Unconscious), FBU (Fake Bad Unconscious), or FBC (Fake Bad Conscious).

In the early 1990s, the two PPI forms were combined: three questions were deleted (that were duplicated), and four added for data collection purposes.

Each seminar given worldwide requires a completed evaluation by the attendee for face validity purposes.

The following reported data has been collected from all of the attendees, on a scale of 1 to 10: 1) personal significance of the seminar. 9.19; 2) professional significance of the seminar. 9.48; 3) accuracy of the profile. 9.07; and 4) competency of the trainer. 9.25.

The Advanced Seminar asks additional phase questions: 1) 97% reported that they had experienced the PTM expected frequent and intense miniscript phase distress sequence in resolving the issue and had phased, and 2) of these, 93% reported that they had experienced the PTM expected issue cover up feeling, and then the underlying authentic emotion, resulting in their phasing.

Of the 700,000 profiled people around the world as of January 2008, approximately 17,000 have been clinical reports.

In the general population, 33% did not phase, 28% phased one time, 20% phased two times, 15% phased three times, 3% phased four times, and only 1% phased 5 times.

Test retest reliability research using the first validated instrument indicates that 85.2% of the time the order of the personality structure remains constant, and that phase order change is predictable.

Appendix E
Study Summaries

For Educators:

Bradley, Dianne, Ph.D. and Smith, Kathryn, Ed.D., September, 1999, Association for Supervision and Curriculum Development, *The Process Communication Model: An Effective Tool To Motivate All Students*.

> Found that when teachers individualize instruction by including motivators for each six Personality Types in every lesson, students learn more, faster and disruptive behaviors disappear or are significantly reduced. Provides suggestions to educators of ways they can stretch to reach every student.

Gilbert, Michael, Ed.D., 1994, Unpublished off-campus duty assignment report, University of Arkansas at Little Rock, *Meeting the Needs of Students Can Promote Success*.

> Found that there was a significant correlation between the interaction energy (similarity in Personality types of teacher and student) and the performance grades of the students.

Gilbert, Michael, Ed.D., 1992, *Dreamers, Rebels, and Others: Personality Styles Affect Communication*, Executive Educator.

> Reported the results of PCM training in the Apache Junction school district over a three year period: – the district reduced employee turnover from 43% to less than 3% (in spite of the fact that the district offered lower salaries than in neighboring districts) – student

achievement in every grade increased dramatically, failure rate in grades seven and eight dropped from 20% to less than 2% – the need for student discipline dropped substantially – graduation rates increased – the percentage of students going on to college or some other kind of post-secondary training increased from 19% to more than 43% – employee satisfaction and morale reached an all time high –parents and students grew increasingly satisfied with school – William Wright was given the Superintendent of the Year Award for implementing PCM.

Hawking, Nancy, Ed.D., 1995, University of Arkansas at Little Rock. Dissertation., *A Study of the Impact on Student Achievement by Teachers Training in Process Communication.*

> Found that teachers trained in Process Communication positively affect student performance through understanding different student Personality Type needs and preferences.

Hopewell, Sylvester, Ed.D., 1997, paper submitted to the Boys & Girls Clubs of Metro Atlanta., *Targeted Outreach Delinquency Prevention Program Assessment*, Research funded by the Bureau of Justice Assistance #4 Grant.

> Found that children in the Boys & Girls Clubs who were exposed to the Kahler PCM program had an enhanced self-concept and greater self esteem. Also, there was overall improvement in morale and camaraderie, an increased involvement in activities, and a desire for recognition for accomplishment.

Knaupp, Jon, Ph.D., Arizona State University (Unpublished paper). *Preservice Teachers' Ranking of Personality Characteristics Preferred by Primary Students, Middle School Students, Parents and Administrators.*

> Found that teachers and students who have differing personality structures will have more miscommunication and the resulting negative coping strategies will be used by both the teacher and student are predictable as a function of their personality typing in PCM.

Martin, Sue, Ph.D., 2001, University of Arkansas at Little Rock. Dissertation., *A Study of the Behavior Causes of Miscommunication in Arkansas Elementary Public School Students.*

> Findings resulted in a statistically significant difference that teachers reading and understanding their own personality profiles, and planning for student differences improved student behaviors.

Wallin, Mark, Ph.D., 1994, Northern Arizona University. Dissertation., *Making the Grade The Effects of Teacher Personality Types on Student Grading Practices.*

> Found that a student's grade is significantly affected by the difference in personality structure between that of the teacher and that of the student.

For marriage counselors:

Shcolnik, Bonnie, Ph.D., 1987, The Fielding Institute. Dissertation., *The Process Communication Model Concept of*

Developmental Processes: The Effects of Phase Development in Husbands on Marital Satisfaction of Wives.

Found that PCM was a useful model for understanding how people might interact in a marital relationship: PCM can predict accurately what a certain Personality Type and Phase individual would experience in a relationship with someone who is a different Personality Type or Phase. Results also point out clearly that PCM is useful in predicting how people will communicate and whether or not specific psychological needs will be issues for them in a relationship.

For alcohol counselors:

Mlinarcik, John, Ph.D., 1990, The Fielding Institute. Dissertation., *Alcoholic Personality Types Revisited a la Kahler's Process Communication.*

Found that Reactive, Type II alcoholics had significantly lower mean Workaholic scores than the matched, nonalcoholic comparison subjects. Results support the movement favoring etiological theories that certain personality and psychological facts may lead to the development of Type II, "Process Reactive Alcoholism."

For school counselors:

Carpenter, Craig, Ed.D., 1994, Arizona State University. Dissertation, *Depressed Children: Brief Intervention Strategies for Teachers.*

Found PCM to be a valuable model for teachers in the understanding of and brief interventions with Reactor Personality Type depressed children.

For mediation:

Johnston, Richard, M.A., 1997, McGregor School of Antioch University. Thesis., *The Value of the Process Communication Mode to a Mediator*.

> Found that PCM allowed the mediator to be in a better position to assess the people negotiating; helped the mediator to identify how each negotiator views their world, understand what preferences each has for interacting with their world, recognize each negotiator's probable distress levels, and motivate each negotiator to behave more in their non-distress way, thus helping to increase each participant's level of clear thinking and good engagement in [completing] the mediation process. PCM also offers the mediator valuable information on what "not" to say or do, and then what and how to say the "best" thing to each negotiator. Furthermore the mediator can use this model to monitor himself/herself for insight into self behavior and a template for making self management decisions.

For therapy:

Nash, Barbara, Ph.D., 1984, Western Michigan University. Dissertation., *Process Therapy: A Reliability and Validity Study*.

> Found that Process Therapy could be a useful and practical model for diagnosis and treatment.

For ADHD:

Bailey, Rebecca, Ed.D., 1998, University of Arkansas at Little Rock. Dissertation, *An Investigation of Personality Types of Adolescents Who Have Been Rated by Classroom Teachers to Exhibit Inattentive and/or Hyperactive-Impulse Behaviors.*

Findings of the study demonstrated statistically significant differences between student personality designations and the inattentive and hyperactive-impulse subscales. The combined findings suggest there were personality characteristics within a student's personality that would predispose him or her toward exhibiting what were perceived by teachers as inattentive and/or hyperactive-impulsive behaviors. Implications and recommendations were suggested for student assignment, for professional development of staff, and for related administrative considerations. The most compelling finding was that miscommunication between teachers and students due to a difference in Personality Type may be the reason many students are referred for and consequently labeled with Attention-Deficit Hyperactivity Disorder. This raises questions about the learning environment, the need to medicate students, and the utility of labels.

Appendix F

Intervening at Second Degree

<u>Thinkers</u>:

Tell them "Good job"
Tell them when it's due
Be organized
Give facts and data – be logical
Be responsible
Acknowledge their hard work
Give rewards and tell why
BE ON TIME
If there is a change in schedule, give them an immediate heads up

<u>Believers</u>:

Tell them "Good job"
Ask their opinion
Listen to them when they give opinions
Always listen
Show RESPECT
Tell them you appreciate their dedication/commitment

<u>Feelers</u>:

Tell them you care about them
Ask about their friends/family
Be sensitive
Genuine compliments about them
Unexpected gifts

Listen to them when they talk about what <u>they</u> want to talk about

<u>Dreamers</u>:

Provide guidelines
Give their own space
Limit tasks to a defined, small set
Give clear priorities
Let them choose their own work space
Provide them time to reflect before asking their views
Give them a heads up about what you are going to want from them

<u>Funsters</u>:

Be spontaneous
Give creative tasks
Make time for fun and humor
Let them customize their work/living area
MUSIC
Toys

<u>Doers</u>:

Make them a deal
Put them in charge of a project
Help them get action
Give tasks involving people
Challenge them
Quick rewards

Person Index

Bailey, Rebecca, 137, 282

Beck, Aaron, 216, 217

Berne, Eric, 1, 2, 3, 4, 5, 10, 11, 12, 14, 16, 25, 29, 45, 53, 62, 68, 103, 111, 112, 113, 139, 142, 143, 144, 197, 226

Berra, Yogi, 17

Boyle, Ron, 17

Bradley, Dianne, 277

Brown, Michael, 183, 263

Bry, Adelaide, 221

Capers, Hedges (Sr.), 1, 5, 8, 12, 16, 29, 107, 144

Chartres, Bernard, 4

Clinton, William (Bill), 18

Clinton, Hillary, 18

Dusay, John (Jack), 26, 30

Einstein, Albert, 10

Ellis, Albert, 218, 219, 226, 227, 228, 230, 231

English, Fanita, 212

Erickson, Erik, 185, 197

Ernst, Frank, 5, 6

Erskine, Richard, 2, 3

Geier, Susan (Sue), 37, 264

Gilbert, Michael, 277

Goodman, Paul, 219, 222

Goulding, Mary, 144, 145, 147, 231, 237, 240

Goulding, Robert (Bob), 144, 145, 147, 231, 237, 240

Groder, Martin (Marty), 112, 113, 223, 224, 226

Hawking, Nancy, 278

Harris, Stuart, 17

Hopewell, Sylvester, 278

Johnson, Luther, 17

Johnson, Richard, 281

Joines, Vann, 30, 31, 32, 35

Kahler, Beau, 17

Kahler, Jason, 17

Kahler, Shirl, 17

Karpman, Stephen (Steve), 5, 10, 11, 139, 140, 143, 144

Knaupp, Jon, 279

Lincoln, Abraham, 244, 245, 246, 247, 248, 249, 265

Lindsley, Ogden, 222

Loria, Bruce, 226

Maris, Robert, 17

Martin, Sue, 279

Maslow, Abraham, 174

McGuire, Terrence (Terry), 241, 242, 266

Mlinarcik, John, 280

Nash, Barbara, 281

O'Hearne, John, 17

Perls, Fritz, 220, 221, 222, 226, 227, 228, 229, 230

Perls, Laura, 220

Rogers, Carl, 117, 118, 226, 228, 229, 230

Roosevelt, Eleanor, 141

Shcolnik, Bonnie, 279

Smith, Kathryn, 277

Steiner, Claude, 104, 106, 144, 147, 226

Stewart, Ian, 31, 32, 33, 35

Stuntz, Edgar (Pete), 1

Wallin, Mark, 279

Ware, Paul, 17, 19, 25, 29, 30, 35, 45, 46, 53, 233, 240, 250, 251, 260

Woollams, Stan, 183